Past
Reality
Integration

Past
Reality
Integration

3 STEPS TO MASTERING THE ART OF CONSCIOUS LIVING

INGEBORG BOSCH
CREATOR OF PRI®

HAY HOUSE
Australia • Canada • Hong Kong • India
South Africa • United Kingdom • United States

First published and distributed in the United Kingdom by:
Hay House UK Ltd, 292B Kensal Rd, London W10 5BE.
Tel.: (44) 20 8962 1230; Fax: (44) 20 8962 1239. www.hayhouse.co.uk

Published and distributed in the United States of America by:
Hay House, Inc., PO Box 5100, Carlsbad, CA 92018-5100.
Tel.: (1) 760 431 7695 or (800) 654 5126; Fax: (1) 760 431 6948
or (800) 650 5115. www.hayhouse.com

Published and distributed in Australia by:
Hay House Australia Ltd, 18/36 Ralph St, Alexandria NSW 2015.
Tel.: (61) 2 9669 4299; Fax: (61) 2 9669 4144. www.hayhouse.com.au

Published and distributed in the Republic of South Africa by:
Hay House SA (Pty), Ltd, PO Box 990, Witkoppen 2068.
Tel./Fax: (27) 11 467 8904. www.hayhouse.co.za

Published and distributed in India by:
Hay House Publishers India, Muskaan Complex, Plot No.3, B-2, Vasant Kunj,
New Delhi – 110 070. Tel.: (91) 11 4176 1620; Fax: (91) 11 4176 1630.
www.hayhouse.co.in

Distributed in Canada by:
Raincoast, 9050 Shaughnessy St, Vancouver, BC V6P 6E5.
Tel.: (1) 604 323 7100; Fax: (1) 604 323 2600

ISBN 978-1-84850-548-3

Poetry on pages 19, 33 and 59 © Vera Bosch www.lifeofmosaics.nl

Printed and bound by CPI Group (UK) Ltd, Croydon, CRO 4YY

The sun is not only the source of light, warmth and life, it has also been a symbol of truth throughout history. In all early cultures the sun is worshipped as a God. Over and over again the sun is revered by man and woman as the essence of life and as the One that shines the light of truth to dispel ignorance and inner darkness.

This book is dedicated to
the divine Spark in our hearts

the water of life
is concealed as a divine gift
inside this body
and that's why you can't see it
the Self has gone and placed
a seal on the heart
and hid love away forever
break the seal
save the love
why are you so afraid?
There are secret paths in the heart
Go and find the beloved
RUMI, 13TH-CENTURY SUFI POET FROM PERSIA

Contents

CONTENTS

Foreword

This book is exceptional. It opens a new way out of our intimate emotional suffering.

Yes, it is a book about psychology, but it does not take the psychological approach we are accustomed to.

As an author myself who for many years has written and reflected on the transformations going on in our society, I consider this book – and Ingeborg's approach to therapy – as more than therapy. I see it *as a way to raise human consciousness.* Her approach is, I believe, new and original.

One could say that PRI [Past Reality Integration] is post-patriarchal and more feminine. Indeed, most of the classical psychological approaches function in a therapist–patient dependency type of relation. Meanwhile, in Ingeborg's approach there is no such dependency relation, as she proposes a toolbox that you can use by yourself in order to heal from many different kinds of suffering, whether on an emotional, physical or even spiritual level. She proposes a three-phase programme which you can apply independently, in the absence of any outside help.

In some cases the help of a therapist might be indispensable, for example in order to work on certain hard-to-discover-by-yourself defences like 'denial of needs' or when you are trying to access deeply repressed and very painful feelings. In those cases, the therapist is more like a coach who enables the transformation of your life. But a coach is not always necessary, as Ingeborg clearly alludes to cases where people have been able to heal themselves, just by applying the PRI method.

This method is also 'transmodern', because it invites you to listen to your body and to your feelings as well as to your intellect. Most of the 'modern' therapeutic approaches have focused on our rational mind. Our modern approach has overstated the intellect and the rational way of looking at things and has underestimated our bodies, our feelings and our intuition. The approach here is more holistic, as it uses the intellect in combination with our intuition and especially our body.

PRI goes further yet, because it invites us to identify which sensation is perceived in our body and to what kind of defence it is linked. In applying PRI our mind *learns* how to communicate with our body. It learns how to ask our body the right questions. The answers our body gives to our mind will *clearly* indicate the way out of our present suffering, which mostly finds its origins in the past. That's what this book is about.

For me, this is a really different approach to therapy, because as a modern intellectual I have not been accustomed to listening to my body, and certainly not to using my body to find the solution to my problems.

At the end of the book the author proposes a very suggestive metaphor, describing PRI as a staircase into light, starting in the basement where there is no light and, quite possibly, one or two skeletons hidden in the cupboards. As a doctor in theology, and a Catholic priest for 12 years, I have gone through the classic Christian spiritual path. But nobody told me about that 'basement' which I needed to clean first. Nobody told me that I should have first healed my wounds of the past. As a result I *appeared* spiritual, but in reality I was nowhere near divine Love. Now, towards the end of my life, I have discovered a way to work efficiently and rather quickly on my own defences, which hide the suffering of my past. And I have discovered that there is no other way to the divine Love within ourselves ... and that experiencing divine Love within myself is possible, if my wounds are healed (at least partly) in the first place ...

This leads us to the final chapter on spirituality. Like Sri Aurobindo and the Mother,[1] Ingeborg is not speaking of religion. She speaks about spirituality and proposes a wise way forward in spiritual growth and higher consciousness.

This book will also interest the younger generations, who are looking for authentic spiritual progress and awakening as well.

In PRI I also feel a close affinity with the Buddhist and the Vedantic[2] invitation to go beyond the ego, which is an illusion. PRI makes this Buddhist and Vedantic vision concrete. It shows that, most of the time, we unconsciously consider sufferings of the past as being really present.

The PRI healing process consists of unmasking this illusion. And this very precise and practical process of unmasking your illusions will lead you to a higher consciousness.

Dr Marc Luyckx Ghisi, 13 July 2010
Member of the International Advisory Board
of Auroville (South India)
Former Member of the 'Forward Studies Unit' of the
European Commission in Brussels
Author

Preface

It is not what happens to us that makes us feel the way we do,
it is how we deal with that which happens.

This book is about a new way of life, a new way of looking at thoughts, emotions and actions so that peace of mind, emotional stability and autonomy can take root in your life.

In three phases and nine weeks you can take the steps that will enable you to use Past Reality Integration (PRI) to change your life. Once you learn these steps you will find that they will provide you with a very practical way to deal with the emotional struggles life challenges you with. You will never again have to feel lost or wondering about how to overcome emotions that negatively affect your life and maybe the lives of those around you as well, preventing you from opening up to the true potential of your life.

After the nine weeks of this programme it will be up to you to free yourself from negative emotions, and shape your life the way you want to. Instead of feeling frustrated or hopeless and alienated from others, you can find that with love and compassion a new connection to yourself, others and life in general is within your reach.

To help you as you apply the different phases of this work, I have devised some extra self-help tools for you. There are the forms that you can download from the

PRI website (www.PastRealityIntegration.com). You can also follow a 'PRI self-help coaching' programme on the website. This is a short practical programme in which the phases described in this book are explained and you get a chance to practise the steps under the guidance of a PRI professional.

Phase 1: Self-observation

When Am I Under the Spell of My Emotional Brain?

As sages from the West and East have been telling us for many centuries, self-knowledge is the beginning of all wisdom. If we don't know ourselves it is very hard to find out what to do about the things that are bothering us. As long as we don't know ourselves we will keep on searching for answers and looking for fulfilment of our desires outside of ourselves. Neither answers nor fulfilment, however, are to be found anywhere but within. In the first few weeks of this programme, aimed at conscious living, I will show you how to install your own 'inner observer'. Once this is in place you will begin to notice those thoughts, emotions and actions that complicate your life and sprout from your 'emotional brain'. This is the part of the brain that acts before it thinks and often generates survival responses. You will discover that when you are irritated or angry it is your emotional brain, not your rational brain, doing the talking. This is also the case when you are feeling afraid, stressed or hyperactive, or when you feel ashamed, guilty or overwhelmed. You will learn that many feelings which you've considered to be perfectly normal, given the circumstances, indicate that your emotional brain has set off an alarm, causing an outdated survival strategy to take you over ...

Phase 2: Symbol Recognition

What Starts Up the Reaction of My Emotional Brain?

Once you are able to recognize the thoughts, emotions and actions generated by the emotional brain, you will learn how to pinpoint the *specific event in the present* that has brought this reaction about (this is the *Symbol*). Often these events seem insignificant at the time, but their impact on our emotional brain can be enough to activate a response which, when looked at more closely, reveals itself to be inadequate at best and destructive at worst. You will learn that the tone in your boss' voice may activate your survival response, causing you to fear her. Or you will discover that you become furious when your children don't look at you when you tell them to do something. Or when you come home from work and you start feeling depressed about your life, this is actually your emotional brain reacting to the fact that your husband has not made dinner yet, as he promised.

All this might sound tenuous to you now, but rest assured that as we proceed through this book it will all become very clear. I will teach you the decoding procedure which will enable you to unravel the messages from your emotional brain, to understand how and why you react the way you do. You will find out that this decoding procedure works in a very simple and precise way – always.

Phase 3: Defence Reversal

How to Reprogramme the Emotional Brain and Live Consciously in the NOW

Once you recognize what has set off your emotional brain, I will show you how to deactivate the survival reaction that follows and which in the present has become totally obsolete. In Phase 2 you will have learned how to decode the meaning of the event that activates your survival response. In this third phase you will learn how to reprogramme your emotional brain. Once you consciously know how to do this, the survival response originating from your emotional brain will only be activated when there is *real* danger in the present and subsequently a *need* for a survival response. When you know how to prevent or stop your emotional brain from reacting in a way that is out of synch with the present, then you will have access to the NOW and experience its surprising lightness and infinite possibilities. 'Living life to the fullest' will become more than just a nice turn of phrase.

For example, when your children don't look at you when you speak to them, you will learn to access the feelings that are hidden behind your habitual angry reaction. You will feel the old pain instead of becoming angry at your children. When the pain passes you will know how you want to address the situation with your children. Not from anger – an inadequate reaction caused by the activation of your emotional brain – but from the perspective of the loving parent you are – an adequate reaction in which your rational brain has had a say as well.

All this will become clear in the following weeks as you go through this book and apply the exercises as described. Step by step it will all start to make sense as you become skilled at recognizing, decoding and working with the feelings, thoughts and actions stemming from your emotional brain. They are reactions that are no longer adequate, no longer needed and very often destructive as well – if not immediately, then inevitably in the long run.

Slowly but surely, the process revealed in this book will lead to a reprogramming of your emotional brain, enabling you to live in the NOW more and more often, consciously shaping your life the way you want it to be. This is quite an exciting adventure which will lead to the unfolding of your true potential – eventually igniting the divine Spark within you.

But first, sit back and take your time to read through the basic theory, in order to fully understand the basics before you get involved in the exercises. You will find this basic theory chapter after the Introduction, in which I share with you my own story and the sources of inspiration life has given me, as well as a first introduction to PRI and its aims. And how the Art of Conscious Living fits into all of that.

Introduction

The Starting Point: A Teenager's Idealism to Change the World for the Better

When I was 15 my mother took me to a workshop on Eastern spirituality. I was immediately fascinated by the concepts that were introduced on video by a man called Jiddhu Krishnamurti. Although I was too young to understand most of what he talked about, I did grab a few notions. Like living in the now instead of living for some goal in the future. That there is only the now, that the past is gone and the future is not yet here. That most of the time we are just filling our time, and in the meantime running away from the emptiness inside. That we create illusions to avoid seeing the truth of our empty lives. That we perceive not the person we love, but the image that we have formed of him or her in our head.

This encounter with Krishnamurti's ideas changed my life. I often see it as the beginning of living consciously. It seemed to me as if I had been asleep until then. It did not go by unnoticed by my friends, either. I idealistically handed out little notes saying 'All this is just an empty pastime.' At home I wondered about the atrocious inequalities in the world and I asked myself 'What is it that makes the average human being tick?' 'Something is really wrong in this world, so what is it and what can be done about it?' I played briefly with the fantasy of leaving it all behind and living on a Greek island, surviving on my daily catch of fish and some minimal amount of cash earned by lodging a few tourists in the summer months. Adolescent daydreaming ...

However, a few years later I decided that leaving society as I knew it would always remain an option but that, before considering leaving, I should at least try to see if I could in some way do something to improve it. That's when I decided to study psychology. I wanted to find out how the mind of the average person works. In those days I still naïvely believed that there was a clear demarcation between the workings of the mind of a 'normal' person and that of someone with a mental illness. I now know better. But back then, I hoped that by studying psychology I'd find out what makes us tick. Once I knew that, I reasoned, I could seriously start thinking about what could be done to improve matters. What naïve idealism, what unruly optimism, what youthful passion to change the world!

As my studies progressed I learned that I was not going to get an answer to my original question 'What makes normal people tick?' Apart from the psychology curriculum, I took a lot of classes on Eastern philosophy (Zen Buddhism, Taoism, Confucianism) and in my final thesis, which focused on applied principles of behaviour modification, I was once more looking for what makes people tick. In a fourth-grade classroom full of children who were interested in anything but paying attention to their teacher and the schoolwork, my co-student and I designed a reward system which after a few months resulted in the kids not only being quiet and listening, but even studying and getting results – without any rewards. That in itself was quite an amazing experience.

After receiving my Master's degree in social psychology I had not yet found the answers I was looking for, nor any clear idea of where to look for them further. As a young consultant I did some work on company culture, but soon discovered that most CEOs want their employees to change and become empowered in the direction they as CEOs think fit. Needless to say this is *not* empowerment. I felt stuck in a moral dilemma. When I truly taught people to become empowered they got in trouble as soon as their ideas were not in line with the ideas of their superiors. But I did not want to pretend, either. The result was that I got out of this line of work and started working as a therapist instead.

I then discovered the work of Alice Miller and, subsequently, that of Jean Jenson and Arthur Janov. Miller's ideas on so-called normal Western upbringing were shocking. She showed how far-reaching the effects are. How the adults we have become are governed to a large extent by the wounds and scars from our childhood. That most of us are not even aware of these wounds that have been inflicted primarily by our parents. And that the results thereof are horrifying. She shows how this applies to extreme examples such as Hitler and Stalin, but just as well to the lives of the unknown heroin addict, the child molester, phobic housewife, depressed sales rep or alcohol-addicted CEO. Childhood suffering is the decisive factor.

Like no other before her, Miller showed how as children we repress pain, and what the effects later in life could be. Her ideas made instant emotional sense to me. She had given the words to that which I had felt for a long time, but had not been able to name because of the collective denial our society finds itself engaged in when it comes to the way we treat children. We don't think twice when it comes to smacking them (words like 'spanking' serve to hide the fact of physical abuse), yelling at them, pushing them, ordering them about and demanding all sorts of things from them including polite and affectionate behaviour, etc. In short, we treat children as if we *own* them, and if they don't co-operate or if we have a bad day ourselves, we feel we have the right to hurt them physically or emotionally 'for their own good'.

After Miller helped me to discover the horrible scenarios taking place in our homes on a daily basis and with nobody thinking anything was amiss, I learned about Jean Jenson's work. While Miller gives very exact descriptions and analyses of what happens to children, Jenson describes a therapy to deal with the effects. Jenson, trained by Arthur Janov in the 1970s, introduced me to her form of Primal therapy. Like Janov, she helped her clients to access the old childhood pain that was locked inside. According to her theory, once felt, this pain would dissolve from our system. I was fascinated by her work and was fortunate enough to meet Jenson and to start working with her. I was then able to put experience and knowledge together and, in 1999, start writing my first book introducing Past Reality Integration (PRI).

While I was writing *Rediscovering the True Self* one of my clients mentioned Daniel Goleman's book *Emotional Intelligence*. Here I discovered the most recent neurological findings, which on a 'brain level' explained the emotional processes I was describing. I was truly amazed. I learned that recent findings had shown that our brain contains an 'emotional brain' and a 'rational brain'. In situations which are unconsciously perceived as threatening, our emotional brain takes over from our rational brain. In order to ensure survival, the emotional brain takes the short route to produce a reaction, instead of the long route which the rational brain would follow. When a car is heading for us we don't have time to evaluate the situation carefully and decide what to do after all options have been duly considered. We just jump out of the way. And we jump before we have even realized we are going to jump. We even jumped before we realized we jumped! Wow, that is the speed of the emotional brain – the speed we need when we are threatened by immediate danger.

The emotional brain can be considered as the storage room of our emotional memory. We might think we are done with the past; but the past is not always done with us. It is our emotional brain which, when activated, links us relentlessly to our past. Thus it can often react to non-threatening situations in the present as if they were threatening situations from the past. PRI shows us why this happens and how we can undo this destructive and often painful mechanism by reprogramming our emotional brain.[1]

So here are the inspirational roots from which PRI grew: Eastern philosophy, behaviour modification, ideas about harmful child-rearing practices, and ways of accessing old pain stored in our bodies. And the whole story turned out to be congruent with the latest research findings in neurology. What a nice discovery.

Many Years Later

Since the publication of the first book on PRI, over 10 years have passed and much work has been done. After

Rediscovering the True Self [2] was published in 2000, *Illusions* [3] came out in 2003, and *Innocent Prisoners* [4] in 2007. Almost 70 therapists are currently trained in PRI, and PRI therapy is now available in English, Dutch, French, German, Italian and Spanish from therapists living in the Netherlands, Belgium and France. The first scientific analysis [5] seems to confirm the good results that practitioners have witnessed, and is very promising. In our practice we see that applying PRI not only reduces the number of negative emotions such as fear and depression, but also substantially improves people's quality of life. Further research in the future is needed in order to determine exactly how effective the results of PRI are. PRI therapists already know that the method is very effective. The results our clients report speak for themselves. Now we have to wait for the first scientific data that can be published.

The Art of Conscious Living

So what is it that we all look for? Happiness? Love everlasting? Peace of mind? Health? Success? All of these at once? As a therapist what I find that people look for most is emotional stability or emotional harmony so that they can make the most of their lives instead of being haunted or pinned down by negative emotions. Most people realize that it is neither possible nor desirable for life to be a bed of roses. No matter how hard we work at our wellbeing, life will always remain unpredictable, and both good and bad things will happen. There is nothing any of us can do about that. What we can do, however, is influence our reaction to all that life brings to us and thereby greatly influence the quality of our life!

I cannot control my children's behaviour, but I can do something about my reaction to it. I cannot make someone love me, but I can influence how I feel about that. I cannot make the traffic jam disappear, or my salary increase miraculously, or the sun shine on a grey day, or everybody to like me, but I can do a lot about how these things affect the way I feel.

Instead of getting angry at my children, I can choose a more constructive approach to reaching them. Instead of being scared of my boss' appraisal, I can develop greater self-confidence. Instead of feeling inferior to my best friend, I can unearth those deep-rooted feelings of low self-worth. Instead of pretending that nothing's the matter, I can open up to my husband and talk to him about my feelings. There are countless examples, but what they all have in common is that the solution to our problems usually lies *within ourselves* and not out in the world. Instead of uselessly trying to change the circumstances and the people around us, we can change the way we react. In other words: if we learn how to reprogramme our emotional brain, we will not be under its spell so often any more. Instead of our emotional brain reacting to the present as if it were the past, we will be able to react from our rational brain *to the present*. And what a difference that makes.

• •

Bill, 45, has always had quite a temper. Behind it he hides a lot of fear. Hidden beneath his large figure and decisive behaviour, nobody notices his vulnerability. Through PRI he discovered that both his overeating and his aggressive behaviour are reactions from his emotional brain. They arise when he unknowingly perceives an event classified by his emotional brain as 'threatening'. In Bill's case this happens every time his wife leaves on a trip or when at work someone seems to ignore him. In these instances Bill's emotional brain registers: 'potential threat of abandonment' and Bill's defence mechanisms set in: eating and becoming aggressive. Instead of feeling that these reactions serve to keep him from feeling the uncomfortable feelings from the past that have been touched off by his wife's or colleagues' behaviour, Bill starts to eat any high-calorie snack he can get hold of, or he becomes verbally aggressive.

After applying PRI to these defensive reactions, Bill effortlessly lost 30 pounds in 6 months; his wife, children and colleagues tell him that he has changed, that he is so much softer, friendlier, has developed an eye for others' needs and is not explosive any more. His doctor informs him that his blood pressure has dropped significantly to a very acceptable level. Bill tells his therapist that these changes have come without trying to eat less, or be nicer or relax more often. These effects have come automatically with the hard work that Bill has been doing to recognize reactions coming from his emotional brain and working with them, instead of blindly giving in to them, rationalizing only afterward that they are 'perfectly normal' and 'just fine'.

Caroline is always trying to please everyone around her. Her friends, her neighbours, acquaintances, anybody in need of some help or a smile could count on Caroline. Except for her husband and children who often saw the other side of her kindness. At home Caroline could be quite easily disturbed and become unfriendly towards her family or dog. Also she had a tendency to drink several alcoholic drinks every day and hide herself behind a book or by watching TV instead of interacting with her family. Inside, Caroline felt empty. No matter how nice she was to people she never felt truly loved or wanted. For a short time, sure. But the good feelings would soon fade and leave her feeling empty all over again.

Through PRI, Caroline learned how she was always on the run – without knowing it – from the emotional neglect she suffered as a child. Any time her emotional brain perceived a chance to get some positive attention and avoid what she interpreted as neglect, Caroline would go running to someone's aid or be her overly friendly self. On the other hand, when she unconsciously felt that the chance for positive attention was small or absent, as was often the case when she was with her family, she would get angry and withdraw from interaction and pour herself another drink.

Once Caroline discovered the true cause of her behaviour, both the so-called positive and the negative behaviour, she could allow herself to feel the pain of childhood emotional neglect still stored in her body, rather than engaging in a defensive reaction. After a while Caroline started to become emotionally independent of others' reactions to her, so she wasn't so eager to please, nor to withdraw or drink any more and her feelings of emptiness started to belong to the past. Both Caroline and her family are very happy about the increase in emotional intimacy they now experience together.

* *

There are yet more dramatic examples, as with the man who discovered that his severe migraines were caused by anger towards his wife. After learning to work with PRI and accessing the pain hidden behind his anger, his migraines disappeared completely. Or the young mother with three children, who knew she shouldn't hit her children but sometimes couldn't control herself. After understanding and working with this very inadequate and destructive reaction, she has never again struck any of her children. Or the woman who suffered from a phobia about driving, who discovered the old pain hidden behind her fear. She worked with it using the tools of PRI and now drives everywhere she wants without being haunted by her old fear for even one minute. Or the man who discovered that his fear of speaking in public covered up a very old pain caused by being physically attacked as a child. He now speaks happily in front of audiences of any size.

I could go on and on with examples of the wonderful and lasting results that have been obtained by using PRI. In therapy it takes an average of 30 sessions to learn to apply the different tools effectively. But many readers have written to tell me how they've succeeded in obtaining results by themselves just by reading my books. These results show me that the time has come to make PRI accessible to a larger audience. Therefore in this book I will try to limit the theoretical and background information to the essential. In my previous books I explain a lot about the background of the method and quote numerous scientific references. In this book I will omit all this 'excess baggage'. Those readers who want to delve deeper into the theory and method of PRI are invited to explore my earlier books.

The essential information is in this book. If you are not bothered by a need to understand exactly all the ins and outs, all the whys and wherefores, this book will suit you fine. I ask you to apply what I am going to teach you, in the order that I describe it and for the minimum amount of time I suggest. Then see for yourself what results are brought about by this kind of conscious living.

The Aim

The aim of PRI is not to change the past, which is of course impossible. The aim is not to feel old pain over and over again. This will only lead to a lot of crying. It will not take away the old pain which we all have stored in our bodies and minds. The aim is not to get rid of all old pain we carry with us. This is neither possible, nor necessary.

The aim of PRI is to start living consciously in such a way that we can change the reaction we have to events in our present lives that somehow unconsciously remind us of the past. These reactions cause us and those around us more harm than good and can even be outright life-threatening. Just think of smoking, drinking, using drugs, eating too much, not coping well with stress, etc. As I've mentioned, our emotional brain can be seen as the storage room of emotional memories. When a present-day event reminds us of an event long gone but stored in our emotional brain, our survival mechanism kicks in without us being conscious of it. We will then defend ourselves from feeling the pain associated by the old emotionally laden memory, shutting ourselves off from our heart and feelings of love and compassion.

By reprogramming the emotional brain we can stop these unconscious defensive reactions from taking place. Then we will be able to react to the present for what it truly is. We will be able to feel what it is we truly need, while simultaneously being in touch with the needs of others.

We are done with the past, and now the past will also be done with us! We can then discover who we truly are. When we start to see through the illusions projected by our emotional brain, our True Self – the divine Spark in our heart – will start to shine forth, liberating us from the prison of defences and illusions that our minds have built. This is the aim of PRI, the method I am going to teach you in this book.

I sincerely hope that it will help you to live your life to its fullest potential, being connected to and guided by the divine Spark that always has and always will shine in your heart.

FRANCE, JUNE 2010

There is only one form of God,
The God that is within you.
Awaken it.
Follow it and realize the truth.
Time rolls by and waits for none,
So start your search while there is still some light,
Before it gets too dark.
SEEMA M. DEWAN, *SAI DARSHAN*

Some Basic Theory

Please take some time to read quietly through this part. I will give you just the essential theory needed to apply the method successfully and reap the benefits. Don't skip this part; you will soon see how essential it is if you want to take your emotional wellbeing into your own hands. If you are interested in a more in-depth approach, as well as scientific and literary references, please refer to my earlier books *Rediscovering the True Self*, *Illusions* and *Innocent Prisoners*.

DIVISION

Due to early childhood experiences everyone's consciousness is divided into three parts: Adult Consciousness, Childhood Consciousness, and the Wall of Denial between them.

In our Adult Consciousness we experience the present for what it is. Unless we are in prison or hospitalized in a closed psychiatric ward, we are aware of the fact that we are independent adults, able to fulfil our own basic needs; we know that nothing lasts forever and that we always have a choice, hard or not, but we do have one. For example: 'I found out my husband has cheated on me. After the shock and a lot of tears, I can feel that I still love him and choose to trust his saying he does not want this to happen again.' Or: 'I found out that my husband has cheated on me. I was shocked and pained, and in the end realized that I don't love him any more. I choose to start a life without him. I know I will be able to find a job and become financially independent.'

Even though the outcomes are opposite, both examples show that these women feel they have a choice and can take their life in their own hands. In short, they are aware that they are fundamentally independent adults.

What we experience when we live from our Childhood Consciousness is quite the opposite. From this perspective we feel that we are dependent on other people to fulfil our basic needs; certain things feel as if they will 'be like this forever', that we can do 'absolutely nothing' about that, and that we do not have any choice but to remain stuck in the unpleasant or sometimes even destructive situation.

To elaborate further on the same example: 'I found my husband has cheated on me. I am in a terrible state. I will die if he leaves me. I cannot live without him.' Or: 'I found out my husband has cheated on me. I hate him for it. I feel terrible. I cannot let the idea of his betrayal go, no matter how often he has told me he is sorry. But I can't leave him, I am stuck with him, he is the breadwinner and I have no marketable skills.' Both of these examples show the lack of perceived choice, the feeling of dependency. These women are unhappy with their situation, but feel stuck, fundamentally feeling unable to take action for themselves. This clearly shows that the 'child perspective' has taken over their view of the present. Because that is exactly how it is for a child: all children are completely dependent on their care-givers; children cannot take care of their own needs; they have no perspective of time and they cannot change the situation by telling their parents to change, nor can they move to the neighbours' in the hope of better care. We all were once small, totally dependent and vulnerable children. Nobody escapes this fact of life.

You might say

Well there is nothing wrong with being totally dependent and vulnerable, because my parents gave me all I ever needed and more. They protected me when I was scared, they listened and understood when I felt alone, they were always happy that I was in their life and they had all the time and energy needed to play with me. Their attention was always available when I needed it; right from the beginning they would always be there to feed me as a baby, never letting me cry by myself in the dark hours of the night. Even when my mother was sick or very tired from taking care of my little brother and sisters, or worried when my father lost his job and suffered from depression, she was still always happy to give me the attention I needed, or to comfort me if I had hurt myself. She never took me to a childminder, and never went away on holiday with my dad until I was old enough to understand time and to know without a doubt that she would come back again soon. She was never upset or angry with me. I truly cannot think of one instance where my basic needs as a child were not lovingly and fully met by my parents.

How idyllic this sounds. And, unfortunately, how unrealistic. As we all know, all adults go through times when they are worried, upset, angry and/or downright exhausted by all the demands life places on us. This is normal life, where we juggle our household duties with the demands of our jobs and the needs of our children, expectations of our family and friends and, if we are lucky, somewhere in that busy schedule we have a few minutes left to ourselves and our partner. Normal life for a perfectly healthy adult does not allow for the time nor the energy always to fulfil our children's basic need for Tender Loving Care.

And what about the life of the adult who suffers from burnout or depression or addiction, or, or, or. The list is long. Approximately 40 per cent of all children grow up with at least one parent who suffers from an emotional disorder, including addiction. Add to this figure all those parents who suffer from physical ailments, like migraines, insomnia, heart disease, cancer, etc. Not to mention the difficult circumstances people face in life such as losing loved ones, losing their jobs, struggling to make ends meet financially, tension within the couple relationship, taking care of sick parents, etc. The list is endless. All of these everyday factors add either directly or indirectly to not being able, as much as we would like, to fulfil our children's basic needs. So as a result babies cry in their cots, children are hit, abused, ridiculed, locked in their rooms or a cellar or cupboard, laughed at when they are scared, ignored when they are sad, not listened to when they are looking for help or upset, forced to eat, yelled at, left alone at home or in bed when they are afraid, neglected, etc. etc.

In short even 'ideal parents' who truly recognize their child's needs – because through personal work they have discovered their own childhood needs – who do not suffer from mental or physical illness, who have a balanced and happy relationship, will sometimes not be able to give their child what he or she needs. And so we are *all* affected.

A child is not able to process the devastating truth that its needs will not be met sufficiently, and will therefore resort to repression and denial of this truth. All those experiences where the small totally dependent child we were did not get its basic needs met, are stored in our Childhood Consciousness. As small and dependent children we were just not able to process events in which our parents did not fulfil our basic needs and there was no one to help us confront this reality. It is simply too threatening to realize that the people whom we were completely dependent upon for our every need were – by definition – not able to meet our basic needs. Not having a perspective of time doesn't make things easier, either: 'Not only am I completely dependent on someone who does not fulfil my basic needs, but this will never change.'

So here repression and denial of this devastating truth kick in. By repressing and then denying the truth, we can keep the threatening experience of being totally helpless and dependent and not getting what we need, out of our consciousness. In order to do this, repression and denial together form a thick wall in between the two other parts of our consciousness. This wall then makes up the third part of our consciousness, which I call the Wall of Denial. Since its function is purely defensive, I also call this wall *the defence system*.

This division of our consciousness into three parts can be represented as follows:

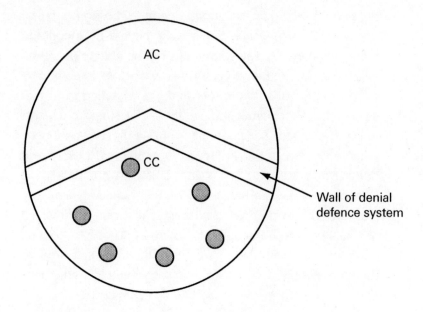

Figure 1 Division of our consciousness into Adult Consciousness (AC), Childhood Consciousness (CC) and the Wall of Denial

OBSOLETE DEFENCES

The middle part – our defence system – has become obsolete and even destructive

However useful and even necessary defences were for the child we were, for the adult we now are these defences are no longer needed. The experiences that as children we could not process are long gone AND we will never be that small, vulnerable or totally dependent child again. We are now adults, independent from others in meeting our basic needs, knowing that all things – good and bad – do change in time and that we always have a choice. *Or have we?*

When our defence system is activated, this adult reality shifts dramatically and we lose the feeling of choice, independence and temporariness. In that case a present-day event is perceived by our emotional brain as a potential danger that needs be warded off at whatever cost. In order to ward off the perceived but illusionary danger, five different defences are available. The dependent child we were *needed* these defences to keep the devastating truth that his basic needs were not met out of his conscious brain. The adult we are now however, has *no need at all* for these obsolete defence mechanisms any more.

There are five different defence mechanisms.[1] When we are children these defences develop one after the other and together they form a healthy psychological immune system: they keep emotionally traumatic events out of full awareness by walling them off in Childhood Consciousness. Or, in other words: they prevent us from becoming fully conscious of the traumatic experience of being totally dependent on our care-givers while they do not meet our needs. Full awareness of this truth would be devastating and even life-threatening, as I mentioned before. So the child who is being neglected will say, 'It is great my parents let me do whatever I like, they trust me.' Or the child who is often hit can think, 'It doesn't hurt me and it is what I deserved.' Or the child who is being abused sexually might say to herself, 'I am Daddy's favourite little girl.' These are examples of denial. Repression is at work when we altogether forget that we were hit, left alone, abused, neglected, etc. or when we forget how often it happened or how bad it really was.

Each defence serves only to keep old pain away from our conscious mind. *It is crucial that we learn to recognize these defences.*

1. Fear

Whenever we feel afraid, nervous, tense, etc. while there is *no* direct physical threat, these feelings are a sign that our emotional brain has kicked in and a defensive reaction has been activated. For example: being afraid to speak in front of an audience. Or being nervous to go to a restaurant or on a trip by yourself. There is no imminent danger, therefore the fear we feel is an illusion. Fear is about threat, about danger. And, however unpleasant it may be, it is not dangerous to eat by yourself in a restaurant or to speak in front of other people.

Fear will make us avoid many things that could make our life more fulfilling and interesting. Our life will reflect this tendency to stay within 'small, predictable limits'. Phobias, panic attacks, chronic anxiety and insomnia are just a few examples of what can be the result.

2. Primary Defence

This defence consists of feelings and thoughts that boil down to the idea that something is wrong with you. These thoughts and feelings can range from 'I am good for nothing, I always screw things up,' to 'I just can't cope, it is all too much for me' to 'Nobody likes me, I am boring,' etc. The common denominator is that every thought or feeling boils down to something being wrong with you. For example when your husband is late for dinner and you think, 'I knew it, I am a bore, I have nothing to say.' Or when your colleague gets promoted and you think, 'See, I am not good for anything, nobody will ever notice my work.' Or when the house is a mess, and the garden full of weeds and the laundry room full of dirty clothes and you feel, 'This is too much for me, I just can't ever get all this work done, I am not able to, I feel overwhelmed.' The Primary Defence causes us to have very low energy levels and a general lack of self-esteem, and can ultimately even lead to a state of clinical depression.

3. False Hope

This defence engenders thoughts, feelings and actions that are usually accompanied by a sense of urgency in situations where there actually is no urgency: 'I *have* to answer this email straight away' when we receive an email; 'I have to clean the whole house before our guests arrive' when we are expecting a visit from some friends; 'I should get the work done now' when there is no deadline. False Hope mostly generates a lot of stress in our lives, causing problems such as insomnia fuelled by ruminating thoughts or perfectionism that exhausts us. It can potentially lead to burnout or substance abuse in an effort to relax our overburdened state of mind. It prevents us from living the life we want to live, since our focus point is outside ourselves. We are predominantly orientated towards satisfying others' expectations or needs as we perceive them, which might not have much to do with their true needs. In the process, of course, we neglect our own needs. False Hope behaviour might give the impression of being about others' needs, whereas in fact it is more about what we get out of it ourselves: appreciation, 'love', recognition, acceptance, etc.

4. False Power

Thoughts, feelings and actions that give off one message: 'Nothing is wrong with me, but everything is wrong with the other person'; any negative thought in which we judge someone else – these are usually signs of False Power. When in False Power we can feel angry, irritated, victimized, jealous, judgemental, critical, etc. All these emotions make it absolutely clear to us that something is seriously wrong with the other person, and we are convinced that the whole world would agree with us. For example, getting angry with your child because you think she should get dressed faster in the morning to get ready for school. Or picking a fight and blaming your wife for her behaviour, instead of listening to her explanation of what happened. Or saying you are not interested in someone's ideas or don't agree with him, without really having explored or understood his opinions. False Power will mostly get us in to a lot of conflicts with other people. It can also contribute to stress-related problems such as migraine headaches and high blood pressure.

5. Denial of Needs

This defence is more difficult to recognize, since on the surface it appears as if there is no problem at all. Actually, it is the *lack* of emotions, or feeling reactions in general, which is the problem. Even in circumstances that would cause most people to feel something, the person who finds himself in a Denial of Needs defence will not feel much at all. It is as if his head and body are no longer in direct communication. The head (mind) is no longer aware of what is going on in the body, both physically and emotionally.

For example: 'A friend just died, and I know I should be feeling sad, but I don't feel anything except for an ache in my stomach.' This man later learned that the ache in his belly actually *was* the sadness that his head 'knew' he should be feeling but didn't.

People with a strong Denial of Needs defence also tend literally to feel less. For example, they will not be bothered much by heat or cold, they won't notice a slight fever they might have, and they are often able to withstand severe physical pain. This can be directly life-threatening, since such a high pain threshold can give doctors the impression that the condition isn't too serious, so they withhold the emergency treatment that might be required.

Another example is 'postponing' behaviour. Since the Denial of Needs defence makes us feel very little, nothing feels very urgent. Postponing or even forgetting things that *do* matter, such as tax forms, bills or what your children or wife have been asking you to do for a few weeks or months now, is quite exemplary of a Denial of Needs defence in action. As is a tendency to avoid taking responsibility. In the Denial of Needs mode, nothing seems to matter much, all seems pretty much OK, so why worry? Being responsible would 'endanger' this fugitive state of being and is therefore avoided.

Denial of Needs is often associated with substance

abuse. The reason is that it is not always easy to maintain the aloofness that characterizes Denial of Needs. In this case alcohol or drugs, but also extended bouts of meditation, sport or watching TV and reading can be of much support in maintaining the comfortable position where 'nothing really gets to me.' Anything that works to anaesthetize the feelings that would otherwise emerge falls within this defence category. As mentioned, the result of an active Denial of Needs defence often will be that it is quite difficult to take on any real responsibility, just as it is difficult to develop intimacy in relationships or friendships altogether. If you lack awareness of your feelings, or have a dulled sense of feeling due to 'anaesthetics', there isn't much of a need for these kinds of things either. 'So why bother anyway, it's just a lot of hassle?'

In the end the result of a strong Denial of Needs defence will be that life passes by without you having lived it. It is like gliding automatically from one year to the next, without ever really coming to what truly matters to you. There's a French expression for this which translates as, 'The "sometime later" alley turns into the "never at all" square.' A terrible shame.

The figure opposite shows how our defences build, layer by layer. Successively, Fear, Primary Defence, False Hope, False Power and lastly Denial of Needs develop into a thick and strong wall that keeps the old pain out of our consciousness.

Since it is crucial to be able to recognize the five defences, please take a look at Appendix 2, which deals in more depth with each defence.

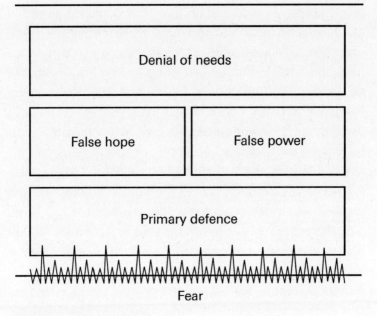

Figure 2 The Wall of Defences

LIVING THE PAST

Present-day events – what I've termed *Symbols* – activate the obsolete defence system, making us live the past without realizing it

Anything that we experience can act as a Symbol and activate one or more of our defences. Something will be a Symbol when it bears a certain, however minute but exact, resemblance to a once-threatening event. These events have been stored in our emotional brain instead of

13

being properly processed so that they could be stored in our long-term memory. This long-term memory is more or less accessible at will. In other words, it contains those memories that we remember consciously: I, for example, remember that I grew up in Persia, that we moved to the Netherlands when I was almost 10 and that I studied in Amsterdam. I do not remember *consciously* how it was to be anaesthetized before I was born, or how my mother held me in her arms the first time she saw me or what it was like when my brother was born. The rational brain cannot process and store adequately until we are about 3 years old. The emotional brain, on the contrary, seems to be up and running even before birth! So a lot of valuable bits of information have found their way to the emotional brain: memories before the age of 3, but also those memories that were too painful for the child to process after that age.

And then, when something happens in our adult life that resembles an aspect of an old painful event that was too devastating for our child self to have fully realized, our defences click in. When we were children this was necessary; it helped us to survive anything no matter how painful as long as it didn't kill us physically. A child will survive severe sexual and physical abuse, emotional neglect and abandonment, because his defence system protects him from fully feeling how devastating his reality actually is.

However, as adults we do not need this protection any more. The supposed threat is not a threat any more. But our emotional brain does not make the distinction in its haste to protect us from possible danger. So, when it detects a resemblance to an old painful event, it activates the defence system and we are stuck with the result: getting

14

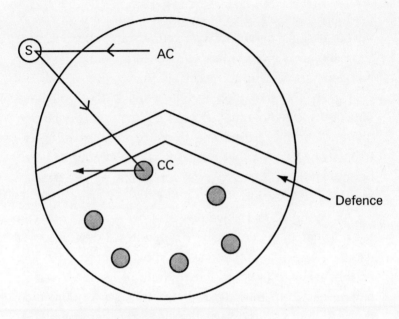

Figure 3 Movement in the Circle of Consciousness

angry, stressed out, afraid, not feeling much or thinking something is wrong with us. And all of that just because our emotional brain jumps to conclusions, the wrong ones!

Let's Do It – All You Need Is 15 Minutes a Day

It is high time to reprogramme your emotional brain so that it stops reacting to perceived threats, which are not threats at all. So that you can liberate yourself from the childhood defence system which dictates large parts of your adult life.

The method is very precise; it has been tested and retested and many, many people including myself have experienced the enormous benefits that are there to be gained.

To tell you the truth, I really wonder where my marriage, my professional career, my health (I was an avid smoker for 16 years) and – even worse – my children would be today if I hadn't applied PRI to myself.

I wish you the good results many before you have obtained and I know that you can do it. You just need one thing: a little bit of discipline to do as is explained in this book *every day* over the coming weeks. Not once or twice or now and then, but *every day* for as long as you need to finish the programme.

All you need is 15 minutes max per day. Nobody can tell me that they can't spare 15 minutes a day. So don't use this excuse to fool yourself! I know you can do it, just as the many PRI clients that I know of could. It wasn't always easy, but they did it and it was worth more than every minute of time they invested! The hardest part is sticking with it, not postponing the exercises (is Denial of Needs your problem?), keeping with it when the going gets tough (some painful feelings will come up, and a few difficult exercises will be necessary) until one day you will start feeling the change in your life. At first it might go by unnoticed, since PRI's effects come from an unconscious level, but sooner or later you will without a doubt notice that your emotional brain is being reprogrammed. That it is not so reactive any more, that it is much calmer most of the time. And if it has a little hiccup, that you will be more and more trained and skilled at calming it down. As a result your relationships will become more harmonious, your children will definitely start to appreciate you much more as a parent, your colleagues and friends will notice you have changed for the better and you will feel more calm, less stressed, not so tempted by substance abuse or overeating, fuelled by love and compassion for yourself and others. You will find yourself in harmony with yourself and your surroundings more and more often. You are mastering the Art of Conscious Living. That is worth investing 15 minutes a day …

Before Beginning – A Promise to Make to Yourself

Make a conscious decision that you want to give yourself this chance to take your emotional wellbeing into your own hands and that you deserve the 15 minutes daily that this will take.

Close your eyes. Breathe in deeply and breathe out as long as you can, three times, and ask yourself:

- *Do I deserve this chance?*

- *Am I going to support myself by taking the required 15 minutes a day?*

- *Every day? Even when it's my mother's birthday or when I've had a bad day at work and I just feel like eating a tub of ice cream in front of the TV?*

If you have answered 'YES' three times, get out a notebook (your only investment) which you will be using for your PRI exercises. Write down:

- *I deserve this chance to take my emotional wellbeing into my own hands.*

- *I am going to support myself by taking 15 minutes to do this every day.*

- *Yes, every day, no matter whose birthday it is or how rubbish I feel about myself.*

- *The only thing needed to make the change I desire is a little discipline so that I can take the required steps every day.*

- *I know I can do it!*

Sign your name and add the date, and then, every day, look at this page briefly before you do your exercises for the day. You are now ready to start Phase 1.

> You might consider reading *Rediscovering the True Self* and *Illusions* (available in English soon) for a more detailed explanation about the PRI theory and method and for scientific and literary references.

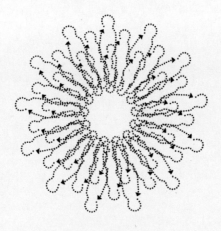

Phase 1
Self-observation

When Am I Under the Spell of My Emotional Brain?

Cut through
The longing
For a better home
Cut through
The resistance
To not feel
How it was
There is nothing to fear
It is just the past
VERA BOSCH, *FULL OF TRUST*

As sages from the West and East have been telling us for many centuries, self-knowledge is the beginning of all wisdom. Only when we know ourselves, our wants and desires, our thoughts, our feelings, the motives behind our behaviour, will we have a chance to do something about the things that are bothering us on a fundamental level.

As long as our mind and feelings are a sort of black box to us, we won't know ourselves and we will keep on searching for the answers to our problems and the fulfilment of our desires outside of ourselves. However, looking for them anywhere else but inside ourselves is doomed to fail. Take a few seconds to really let this sink in. Yes, only inside yourself will you find the answers to your problems and the way to the fulfilment of your desires. Anything that comes to us from the outside will at best give only temporary relief, happiness or joy, but it won't last!

Get to Know Your Personal Defence Profile

Before you start the exercises belonging to Phase 1, it is helpful to know which defences you use most. Take the test in the back of this book – Appendix 1. Most people enjoy finding out more about themselves by taking tests like this. Maybe your partner or a friend would like to take it as well. Doing this kind of work together always helps tremendously in sticking with it.

The test will show you whether you mostly use Fear, Primary Defence and False Hope (a profile more prone to depression) or a combination of False Power and Denial of Needs (a profile with little emotional intimacy in relationships), or that maybe you often combine False Hope and Denial of Needs (a profile that is at high risk of perfectionism and burnout, or other 'energy-deficiency' illnesses such as fibromyalgia, chronic fatigue syndrome/ ME, RSI), or that you fall into the category of people who are strong on False Power and the Primary Defence (feeling victimized is strong in this profile, as well as what are called borderline personality traits), or any other combination of defences.

If you have low scores all over (4 or less on each defence) this means that you have either already done a lot of personal development work and you can stop reading now, or – more likely – it means that you have an enormous Denial of Needs defence. Actually, since Denial of Needs prevents you from feeling much at all, most questions in the test will not seem relevant to you. If this is the case, take extra care not to lose the perseverance needed to finish the programme.

Taking the test will help you to get a better idea of the kind of thoughts, emotions and behaviour you are looking for in Phase 1, during which you want to get a good picture of when your defences are activated.

Installing the Inner Observer

As mentioned in the Preface, in the first few weeks of this programme I will show you how to install your 'inner observer'. Once this is done you will begin to recognize those thoughts, emotions and actions that complicate your life and sprout from your emotional brain.

As discussed earlier, this is the part of the brain that acts before it thinks and often generates survival responses. You will discover that when you are irritated or angry it is your emotional brain talking and not your rational brain. Just as is the case when you feel afraid, stressed or hyper, or when you feel ashamed, guilty or overwhelmed. You will learn that many feelings you thought were perfectly normal under the circumstances might not be so adequate and 'normal' after all. You will discover how they indicate that your emotional brain has set off an alarm causing an outdated survival strategy to take you over.

Recognizing Your Defences

During the next two weeks – or as long as you need to get a feel for it – I am going to ask you to observe your feelings, thoughts and reactions. The objective is to recognize any reactions that fall into one of the five defence categories:

1. *Fear: being afraid, tense, nervous, etc. when there is no immediate physical danger. An example of this might be: 'I am afraid to go to a party by myself,' 'I am afraid to tell my friend I don't like the way he treats my wife,' 'I am afraid on aeroplanes,' 'I can't sleep in the dark by myself,' etc.*

23

2. *Primary Defence:* any thought or feeling about yourself that is negative. For example: 'I am bad,' 'I am guilty,' 'I can't do it' – or any variation of these thoughts.

3. *False Hope:* a sense of urgency, stress, feeling that 'it' (the False Hope behaviour) has to be carried out, the idea that if you changed, things would be OK. Often False Hope involves doing what you think will please other people. For example: 'If I am more this or less that, it will be all right,' 'If I reply to her accusations in the right way, she won't be angry any more,' 'If I am a perfect mother, my children will be happy and love me,' 'If I lose weight, all my problems will be over,' etc.

4. *False Power:* irritation, anger, fury or any other emotion or judgement saying that there is someone else who is bad, wrong, guilty, etc. For example: 'He disgusts me, why can't he stop drinking?' 'Don't count on him, he is a loser,' 'I don't want to have any contact with you any more, something serious is wrong with you,' 'I can't stand her, she is successful, intelligent, nice and good-looking,' etc.

5. *Denial of Needs:* a general flatness of feeling, forgetfulness, procrastinating, acting as if there is no problem when there is, not needing anything, being easy-going, acting like everything is fine, not having a passion in life, substance and food indulgence, being a workaholic, etc. For example: 'Sure, I'm fine, and you?' – just after divorcing; 'Oh, I will take care of that later' – the lightbulb has been broken for weeks now;

'I don't care what we do, everything's fine with me,'
'Don't worry about me,' etc.

If you would like additional explanation and further examples of the five different defences before you feel competent enough to start the search for your own, please read Appendix 2 or go over the basics (page 8) once more.

You can also check your capacity to recognize the defences by taking the defence recognition test in Appendix 3. And of course in my book *Illusions*[1] you will find detailed information about each defence.

You are now well prepared to take the first step. Think of it as a sort of treasure-hunt: the PRI 'defence-hunt'. Looking at tracking down your defences as an interesting yet somewhat playful challenge that will not only teach you a lot about yourself, but make the process fun as well along the way.

If you are doing this programme together with a partner or friend, you could make it into a game about who recognizes the most defences in a day. Remember we all, yes all, have many, many defensive reactions every day.

WHAT YOU DO IN PHASE 1

Make sure that you always have a few post-its and a little pencil with you, both small enough to fit into your pocket or handbag. Make sure that you wear clothes with pockets during the whole duration of this programme.

Self-observation 'Post-its'

Each day (yes each day, remember?), look for any defensive reactions you might have. Just observe your behaviour, thoughts and feelings.

Do you think you have recognized one of the five defences? If so, jot down *just a few words* on a post-it. This will help you to remember later on that day what was happening at the time that you recognized a defence. You need this for the second part of the work in this phase. More important, jotting this down will help you to anchor the experience of recognizing a defence. This will help you to catch more and more defences, quickly and easily. In time it will be as if a little buzzer starts buzzing when a defence kicks in. And this will make it a lot easier for you to recognize when you have been taken over by a defensive reaction. Recognizing this fact forms the entire basis of PRI work.

Don't worry if this is hard in the beginning, just stick with it and you will see that after a while you will start to become quite skilled at it. It will hardly take up any extra time at all. The idea is to live your life as you have always done, just write down a few words every now and then, when you suspect a defence has got the better of you.

For example, this could be a typical day's 'harvest' for a person we'll call Mary:

- *Bob/tea*

- *Andrea/TV/couch*

- *Joe/we all*

As you can see these are lists that make sense to no one except the person who has written it down. When reading over these notes, however, the person who made them will remember the situation clearly straight away. And that is just what is needed later on in the day, as will be described shortly.

In this example, 'Bob/tea' refers to the situation where Mary notices her husband Bob drinking tea. Even though Mary has always liked tea, Bob rarely drinks tea with her, preferring coffee or beer. Now that he has a new friend who drinks tea often, Bob himself is also starting to drink tea more often. This brings on irritation in Mary, clearly a defensive reaction. Mary recognizes the defence, takes her PRI notepad and pencil out of her pocket and writes down 'Bob/tea'. In the next section I will explain to you how she – and you – proceed from here.

Self-observation Analysis

Here's where the 15 minutes a day come in. Copy the Self-observation Analysis Form shown on page 29 onto an A4 size piece of paper, or make a printout of the form available online (www.PastRealityIntegration.com). File these forms in a folder so you can keep track of your progress.

Find a *set time every day* that is convenient to you to write out the observations you've made during the day. For most people this will be in the evening right after dinner, or somewhere in the morning before beginning the work day. Just before going to bed doesn't work out very well in general, because most people feel too tired by that time to concentrate. See what suits you best. When can you best give yourself the daily 15 minutes needed to start up a new way of life?

Once you find the time best suited to your schedule, needs and energy level, *stick to it*. Having a set routine will just make it a lot easier to maintain the discipline needed to complete this programme successfully, so that thereafter you will be able to live more consciously, taking your life and your wellbeing into your own hands.

Fill out the Self-observation Analysis Form to analyse what has happened during the day. You can do this by hand or on your computer, whatever suits you best. Just as long as you take those 15 minutes a day to fill it in. Look at the *self-observation notes* you've made that day and, for each situation, write down *briefly* (this is not a diary):

- Situation: *the situation in which you became defensive*

- Reaction: *what your reaction was*

- Defence Category: *which defence category that reaction belongs to.*

If you have recognized many defences that day, just analyse however many situations you can on your form in the allotted 15 minutes. Don't worry if you can't do them all. You'll get the practice you need in 15 minutes as long as you do it every day. Also note the date and number of your analyses. This will give you an idea of the quantity and regularity of your work, two decisive factors in making PRI work for you.

Self-observation Analysis Form – Phase 1

Date	No	Situation (S)	My Reaction (R)	Defence Category (D)

EXAMPLES

Date: 11/2

No. 1

S: Bob drinking tea

R: saying 'You like tea all of a sudden?' and feeling irritated

D: False Power

Date: 12/2

No. 2

S: my boss not including me in the email about Carla's illness

R: pushed away the uneasy feeling this brought up by keeping on working

D: Denial of Needs

Date: 12/2

No. 3

S: sound of doors slamming in the house

R: afraid to go and find out what is going on

D: Fear

Date: 13/2

No. 4

S: email from Sue about our last conversation

R: uneasy feeling, it's not true what she says about me, she interpreted my words incorrectly

D: False Power

Date: 13/2

No. 5

S: depressed sound of Tristan's voice on the phone, after he got angry at me last night

R: put on a nice friendly voice, hoping he's not mad at me any more

D: False Hope

Date: 14/2

No. 6

S: Sue's mail – I didn't do my homework

R: irritation which I didn't show

D: False Power

Date: 14/2

No. 7

S: working on my homework

R: thinking 'I can't do it, it's going to be zero'

D: Primary Defence

Date: 14/2

No. 8

S: Sandra's remark 'Why do you always choose sides?'

R: thinking 'I'm not of any worth at all'

D: Primary Defence

If you have a good friend or partner who is interested in this approach as well, it can really help to do the programme together. It will be a lot easier to stick to your daily 15 minutes of work when you know that you will be talking about it with someone else. And you will have someone to share your experiences with. Meet once a week, evaluate how you are doing, discuss difficulties and help each other discover blind spots.

In the beginning you will most likely find just one or two situations a day in which you recognize your defences at work. Don't worry. We are all *so very, very* used to seeing these defensive reactions as perfectly normal – 'I have been like this all my life, it's my character, and besides it runs in the family, so it must be genetic.' Just keep going, reminding yourself to watch out for any reaction that might be defensive, writing it down and analysing it later on. Sooner than you think, you will get the hang of it. Once you are able to recognize around five defensive reactions per day, you are ready to go on to Phase 2. Most likely you will need about a fortnight to get that far.

Don't cheat by going to Phase 2 too quickly. If you can't recognize your defences it is impossible to do PRI. Leaping ahead of yourself will not help you to get results any faster. In fact it will do just the opposite. The better you get at recognizing your defences, the better your results will be. Any extra investment that you make in this phase is worth twice the effort. So be patient, observe yourself all day long, make notes and fill out your Self-observation Analysis Form every day for a maximum of 15 minutes. When you have no trouble noticing five or more defences a day, then you can move on to Phase 2.

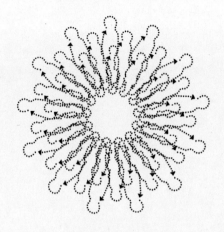

Phase 2
Symbol Recognition

What Starts Up the Reaction of My Emotional Brain?

Did you ever love so intensely
That you would condemn yourself to hell eternally?
I have …
Hoping for a better life
Fighting for my rights
Not feeling the deep longings inside
Have you ever loved so deeply
That you have given yourself for that dream?
So you did not have to feel
How empty and lonely it once was
VERA BOSCH, *TO LOVE*

Once we are able to apply Phase 1 and we can recognize the thoughts, emotions and actions generated by the defences set off by our emotional brain, it is possible to take the next step on our way to the Art of Conscious Living: finding the specific event in the present that brought this reaction about.

Sometimes these events stick out like a sore thumb; often, however, such events go by almost unnoticed at the time. Their impact on our emotional brain, though, is undeniable, since an emotional response is activated. An emotional response which, when looked at more closely, reveals itself as inadequate at best or, more often, as downright destructive.

For example, you will learn that it is a look on your mother's face that activates your survival response of becoming afraid of her (Fear defence). Or you will discover that you become furious (False Power defence) when your husband forgets to ask you how your day was. Or when you come home from work and you start feeling depressed about your life (Primary Defence), it is actually your emotional brain reacting to the fact that your children have not hung out the washing.

In this phase I will show you the PRI 'decoding' procedure, which will enable you to unpick your emotional reactions to understand how and why they occur. In this phase you will also find out how this decoding procedure works in a very precise way – always.

WHAT YOU DO IN PHASE 2

Self-observation Post-its and Self-observation Analysis

The structure of Phase 2 is the same as that for Phase 1.

First of all, you continue noting down a few words on your PRI post-its as soon as you recognize a defensive reaction. Don't delay, because you really need to anchor in your brain the experience of recognizing a defence.

Then, just as in Phase 1, once a day you sit down for a maximum of 15 minutes to fill out the Self-observation Analysis Form. Remember you can copy the form from this book onto an A4 piece of paper, you can also download the Phase 2 form directly from the PRI website.

Finding the Symbol and the Sensory Perception

In the second step of Phase 2, I am just going to add a few ingredients to the work you have been doing so far.

First of all, as I've mentioned, the situation that activates your defensive reaction is what we call a *Symbol*. It is called a Symbol because it is symbolic of something that happened in your childhood which was too painful for you to have processed properly. As a result the painful memory remains stored in your emotional brain.

Symbols are all those present-day events, people, experiences – all that we perceive consciously or un-consciously – that show a very specific resemblance to a painful event stored in our emotional brain. Consciously we are *not* aware of this resemblance, it is only by becoming aware of the fact that our reaction is a defensive one that we can *deduce* that we must have been affected by a Symbol.

A Symbol can be just about anything: the people in your life, but also a piece of music, a movie, or even the sight, sound or smell of something. Just about anything can be a Symbol, as long as it contains a *very specific* detail that resembles an old painful situation.

It is as if we are walking around with a little webcam on top of our head. This camera continuously scans our environment for anything that might be a threat to us. As soon as it detects something in the present that resembles an old event stored in our emotional memory, the defence system is activated.

In Phase 2 of the programme you will find out what exactly it is about the Symbol that makes your emotional brain sound the alarm. Finding this exact point, which I call the Sensory Perception (SP), will make it possible to access your emotional brain and thereby – in Phase 3 – enable you to reprogramme it so that it will react to the present instead of the past.

You can get to this exact point, the so-called Sensory Perception, by asking yourself the following question:

What exactly did I perceive with my senses (usually by seeing or hearing, but smell, taste and touch are possible as well) the moment that the defence was activated?

For example: you feel anger coming up the moment your friend accuses you of something and doesn't listen to what you have to say about it. This is clearly a feeling showing that a defence has been activated (False Power, to be exact). The Symbol is easy to find as well – it's your friend. But what is the Sensory Perception that made your emotional brain take over?

Go back to the Symbolic Situation in your mind's eye. See the scene in front of you again.

- *What exactly did you perceive* just before *you got angry?*

- *What was it that got to you* most?

- *What is the* first *thing that comes to mind when you put yourself back in the Symbolic Situation?*

- *Imagine looking at your friend's face again. Listen to her words again. What comes at you right away?*

- *Focus all your attention.*

The answer could well be: 'The strong expression of judgement and disapproval on her face: piercing eyes, corners of the mouth turned down'. The answer could also be: 'Her words "I don't believe what you are saying,"' or 'The loud voice and aggressive tone in her voice'.

It is up to you to go back to the Symbolic Situation, close your eyes if that helps to imagine it more vividly, and find what it is that comes at you *first*. This is usually the specific aspect of the Symbolic Situation, the Sensory Perception (SP), which has activated the reaction from your emotional brain.

The way you describe the Sensory Perception does not have to be that which happened literally. We are talking about what *you* perceived – and that is, by definition, subjective. So don't worry whether what you perceived was correct or not. Just try to get a clear picture, sound, taste or smell of what *you* perceived. Just realize that what you are doing here is gaining access to your emotional mind. And what happens there is about only one person – *you*, and nobody else. Fully realize that what you perceive about a person or situation that is a Symbol to you says a lot about you and *little, if anything at all*, about the present reality.

Later on we will get back to the present reality and whether there is a real need to do anything in the now. Just 'use' your Symbol as a doorway into your emotional brain and a way out of your defensive life!

Practise finding the Symbol and the Sensory Perception for about two weeks before you move on to the next part of this phase. Continue your 'defence-hunt' during the day (just as you did in Phase 1) – the more defences you are able to hunt down, the bigger the treasure that you will find in the end – and add the Sensory Perception and Symbol to your Self-observation Analysis Form, as shown overleaf:

Self-observation Analysis Form 1 – Phase 2

Date	No	Symbolic Situation (SS)	My Reaction (R)	Defence (D)	Sensory Perception (SP)	Symbol (S)

EXAMPLES

Date: 1/12

No. 1

SS: email from Joe about his training programme

R: I feel annoyed, but react in a friendly way

D: False Power (only note the first defence you recognize – in this example, False Power, signalled by annoyance, which is then covered up by acting in a friendly way, which indicates False Hope)

SP: his written words: 'you reacted unpredictably'

S: Joe

Date: 2/12

No. 2

SS: my electrician saying he doesn't know if he disturbed the wires of my internet connection

R: I feel very annoyed and tell him that he should know what he is doing

D: False Power (this one is easy, no attempt to cover it up this time)

SP: the blank and 'lost' look on his face

S: the electrician

This one needed a little more thought. At first glance it would be easy to think that the Sensory Perception consisted of his words: 'I don't know.' But as this person went back to the Symbolic Situation and saw it again, the *first* thing that came to him was not the electrician's words but the expression on his face. That's how you recognize the Sensory Perception: usually the *first* thing that comes to mind or the thing that you feel has the most emotional charge attached to it when you let yourself go back to the Symbolic Situation.

Date: 3/12

No. 3

SS: on the phone talking to my sister, she signals that she doesn't like what I've said

R: I feel fearful of being misunderstood and rejected, I remain silent

D: Fear

SP: my sister saying 'I don't feel good about talking to you about this subject'

S: my sister

Whether your sister said these exact words or not, they are what come back to you when you go back to the Symbolic Situation. And that is what matters, what comes back to *you*, not what did or didn't happen in reality, was said or wasn't said. Remember, this is about *your* emotional brain and its hidden contents, not about finding out what is happening in the NOW. That part comes later.

Date: 4/12

No. 4

SS: inviting my husband and daughter, who are reading on the couch, to come and read in bed with me, and their refusal

R: I say, 'Oh, that's OK' and go and read in bed by myself

D: Denial of Needs

SP: my husband saying 'I am reading my book here with Anne'

S: my husband

How do you know that a Denial of Needs defence was involved? It didn't seem like a big deal, you said it was fine that they stayed where they were, but ... if you are really, really honest with yourself, there was a little twinge in your stomach the moment your husband refused your invitation. Just before you nonchalantly said, 'Oh, that's OK,' you felt rejected and disappointed that he didn't react with warmth and enthusiasm.

Body Awareness

When you start out doing this work, it will be hard to realize that there is something going on for you when at first you seem to be 'just fine'. This is where your body awareness comes in.

If you are tuned in to your body's signals you will be able to discover that something *is* going on for you, including in more subtle situations like in the example above. However, many of us have lost this awareness of our body's more subtle signals. If you find that you have difficulty in recognizing almost any Symbolic Situation, this might be your problem. In that case I advise you to read Appendix 4 where I share with you some breathing techniques that can be of great help in reconnecting with your body.

It is not surprising that many people have a hard time connecting to what their body is trying to tell them, since as children most of us were brought up with 'Don't make a fuss,' 'Shut up and do as you're told,' 'Don't be such a cry baby,' 'You're a spoiled little brat,' 'Boys don't cry,' 'I'll give you something to cry about,' etc. All these messages teach children from a young age that they should repress their emotions, or at any rate it teaches them not to show their emotions and eventually not even to feel them. The main result of this 'training' is that we lose our connection to the signals our body sends us.

The good news is that this connection can be restored, and a most effective way to do it is through breathing exercises (see Appendix 4).

Please give yourself the time to reconnect with your body if this connection is not self-evident to you. Attempt this Phase 2 step of finding the Sensory Perception once you feel you are in touch with your body. Remember, you are on your way to mastering the Art of Conscious Living by taking your emotional wellbeing into your own hands. Then living your life to its fullest potential becomes well within your grasp!

A few more examples of the second step of Phase 2, finding the Sensory Perception:

Date: 5/12

No. 5

SS: hearing sounds in the hallway while I am watching a video on my computer

R: I have a startled response and hope my husband will not come in and find out I am not working, I sit quietly and wait

D: Fear

SP: sudden sound in the hallway

S: my husband

Date: 6/12

No. 6

SS: my son is home for lunch and sits in the kitchen

R: I want to ask him about his girlfriend but I don't say anything, thinking he doesn't want to talk to *me* about it.

D: Primary Defence

SP: his not looking at me, but gazing at the floor

S: my son

Here we see that even though the defensive behaviour is about avoidance, which usually comes from fear, it isn't the Fear defence that has been activated, but the Primary Defence. You can be sure about this because the 'reasoning' for the behaviour is 'he doesn't want to talk to *me*' – implying a negative self-judgement and not so much a fear. It would have been fear if you had felt something like: 'I won't say anything because he'll get angry with me.' Then the focus would be on possible anger coming towards you and the fear in reaction to that. But in this example the focus is on the negative self-perception, so it is a Primary Defence reaction.

Date: 7/12

No. 7

SS: my friend not inviting me in for some tea

R: behaving completely as if nothing unusual has happened, not mentioning tea

D: False Hope

SP: her friendly 'business as usual' behaviour

S: my friend

In this case you could easily think that the defence was Denial of Needs and not so much False Hope. However, while behaving 'normally' it was clear to you that you didn't feel 'just fine' about the situation. Not saying anything about it was not so much due to not feeling anything, which would indicate a Denial of Needs. In this case not saying anything was about trying to hide the feeling of rejection and to be nice to her so she would not be annoyed with you. So here we see a False Hope defence operating.

Date: 8/12

No. 8

SS: my mother telling me that my father reacted negatively to the talk we had

R: I try to justify what I said by blaming him, but underneath it I feel guilty and I end up sending him a nice email

D: Primary Defence

SP: my mother saying about my father: 'He has to think about it, what you said really affected him deeply'

S: my father

Here again you can see the way in which the defences follow one another. First there is the feeling of guilt covered up by justifying behaviour, then False Power looms and you say that he is the one who is wrong after all, and finally you clean it all up with a nice email to buddy up to him again! False Hope. What elaborate strategic manoeuvres, albeit unconscious ones!

Date: 9/12

No. 9

SS: my therapist tells me that he thinks that my wanting to record the session could stem from a desire to control

R: I try to explain why recording works well for me, but I feel insecure in doing so

D: Primary Defence

SP: his overpowering energy when he says this to me

S: my therapist

Date: 10/12

No. 10

SS: I look at my watch and realize I am going to be too late for my dental appointment

R: I say, 'Oh no, he's going to be upset'

D: Fear

SP: the dentist's angry face when I get there

S: the dentist

In this situation a person who is not there at the time the defensive reaction is activated *is* nevertheless the Symbol. Normally the Symbol and the Sensory Perception, which is always part of the Symbol, are both present at the time our defences are activated.

In some cases, however, and quite often in the case of the Fear defence, we might be reacting to something that we foresee happening in the future. In that case it is the image that we see in our mind, and not the reality, which acts as a Symbol.

Finding the Meaning

Once you have become somewhat skilled at finding the Symbol and the Sensory Perception, we arrive at the third part of Phase 2: finding the meaning.

This third part of Phase 2 is very important since it will give you a clear idea and sense of the old repressed pain and the reality of the child you were. Both the old pain and the old reality are touched upon by a Symbol.

Ask yourself: *What does this Sensory Perception mean to me? What message do I feel the Symbol is actually giving me? What, in my eyes, is the Meaning behind the Sensory Perception?*

The Meaning is actually a *direct reflection* of our Old Reality – all those experiences that we as children could not process properly because they were too painful.

There is nobody except *you* who can put the Meaning behind the Sensory Perception into words. Think of the famous saying 'beauty is in the eye of the beholder' and exchange the word 'meaning' for beauty. That is what this step of PRI is about. You are accessing *your* emotional brain, and you are the only one who can know whether that has been done successfully or not.

You will know by the emotional reaction that follows once you find exactly the right words: if you feel nothing, you know it's not right – you have not found the Meaning, the exact reflection of your Old Reality. If you feel sort of bad, you are getting close but you are not there yet. Only if you feel a *sudden and sharp* emotional reaction do you know that you are exactly on the dot. And only in that case is this method going to *help* you – it's either right on the dot or not. If it isn't, it will not help you to access your old pain which was touched upon by the Symbol and then quickly covered up by your defences.

When you get to the correct Sensory Perception and Meaning attached to it, you will feel as if stung by a bee: a *sudden and sharp* emotional reaction. In my other books this is why I refer to the Sensory Perception and the Meaning together as the 'sting': it really stings you like a bee if you get it right.

Keep in mind that the Meaning is the message conveyed by the Sensory Perception. In other words, the message that you feel is coming at you from the Symbol. It is *not* your judgement of the Symbol. When you judge you are looking *at* the Symbol and evaluating it, putting into words what you think about the Symbol: 'he is aggressive,' 'he is useless,' 'she is in denial,' etc. Looking at the Symbol like this will most likely generate a False Power (judgement) reaction. *This is not going to help you!*

Instead of judging and evaluating the Symbol and your Sensory Perception, see the Sensory Perception *coming at you*: what is the message coming at you, what is the Meaning coming *at* you? The False Power idea 'he is aggressive' then might transform into 'I am going to destroy you.' The 'he is useless' False Power idea might change into 'I am not going to help you, no matter how much you need me,' etc.

Can you *feel* the difference, as you read this? The judgemental position generates irritation or anger. On the other hand, the perspective where you let the Meaning come *at* you touches on old pain directly while *dissolving any tendency to judge*.

As long as you feel any inclination to judge the Symbolic person or situation, you are still caught up in your False Power defence and not in touch with the Meaning. *This is very important to keep in mind*.

You really don't want to build up your False Power by applying PRI incorrectly.

Setting the Symbol Free ...

Remember that you will only be able to admit that you are in defensive mode, enabling you to apply PRI and work with the Symbol, if you are willing to let the Symbol 'off the hook'. This means that you consciously accept that once someone or something is a Symbol, that you are incapable of knowing what is really true about the Now. If you are caught in the Primary Defence, thinking that your friend doesn't want to see you any more because she didn't get in touch with you, you are not capable of judging whether her silence indeed means that she doesn't want to see you any more. It is the Primary Defence that whispers – or, rather, shouts – that idea into your ear. In this way each defence colours our perception of the reality, and our interpretation of it. Therefore, avoid any declarations about the present once you feel that you are in the grip of one of your defence mechanisms.

This takes a lot of discipline, since our whole defence system aims at convincing us that something is going on in the present with the Symbol!

If you want to work with PRI and master the Art of Conscious Living, there is only one thing you can do and that is to set the Symbol free: not making any judgements or evaluations. Later, after Phase 3 and when the emotional charge is gone, you will be able to look at the Symbol with compassion and know what is true for you, NOW. You will have accessed and reprogrammed your emotional brain, taking away the old emotional charge that was stuck to the present. *It is absolutely impossible to do this if you keep insisting on your judgement or evaluation of the Symbol, or, even worse, if you deny something is a Symbol at all for you and insist on passing judgement!* We all know that 'hardened' feeling we get when we judge or condemn something or someone. We are absolutely sure the other really is not OK, or has done something really wrong. From whatever angle we look at it, we just cannot come to any other conclusion.

In these kinds of situations, try to remember – even if it is only with one tiny brain cell – that any judgement is an expression of False Power and that you are just short-changing yourself when you allow yourself to be dragged off by that defence, and then I am not even mentioning what you are doing to the other person. Set the Symbol free and concentrate on applying the PRI steps!

Self-observation Analysis Form 2 – Phase 2

Date	No	Symbolic Situation (SS)	My Reaction (R)	Defence (D)	Sensory Perception (SP)	Symbol (S)	Meaning (M)

So let's look at the previous examples I gave and add on the Meaning which the Sensory Perception will have had for your emotional brain.

Date: 1/12

No. 1

SS: email from Joe about his training programme

R: I feel annoyed, but react in a friendly way

D: False Power (only note the first defence you signal)

SP: his written words: 'you reacted unpredictably'

S: Joe

M: 'I don't want to have anything to do with you any more'

Date: 2/12

No. 2

SS: my electrician saying he doesn't know if he disturbed the wires of my internet connection

R: I feel very annoyed and tell him that he should know what he is doing

D: False Power

SP: the blank and 'lost' look on his face

S: the electrician

M: 'I cannot give you what you need'

Date: 3/12

No. 3

SS: on the phone talking to my sister, she signals that she doesn't like what I've said

R: I feel fearful of being misunderstood and rejected, I remain silent

D: Fear

SP: my sister saying 'I don't feel good about talking to you about this subject'

S: my sister

M: 'I don't want to be with you any more'

Date: 4/12

No. 4

SS: inviting my husband and daughter, who are reading on the couch, to come and read in bed with me, and their refusal

R: I say, 'Oh, that's OK' and go and read in bed by myself

D: Denial of Needs

SP: my husband saying 'I am reading my book here with Anne'

S: my husband

M: 'I couldn't care less about being with you; I want to be with her'

Date: 5/12

No. 5

SS: hearing sounds in the hallway while I am watching a video on my computer

R: I have a startled response and hope my husband will not come in and find out I am not working, I sit quietly and wait

D: Fear

SP: sudden sound in the hallway

S: my husband

M: 'I can do anything to you that I want'

Date: 6/12

No. 6

SS: my son is home for lunch and sits in the kitchen

R: I want to ask him about his girlfriend but I don't say anything, thinking he doesn't want to talk to *me* about it.

D: Primary Defence

SP: his not looking at me, but gazing at the floor

S: my son

M: 'I don't want to have anything to do with you'

Date: 7/12

No. 7

SS: my friend not inviting me in for some tea

R: behaving completely as if nothing unusual has happened, not mentioning tea

D: False Hope

SP: her friendly 'business as usual' behaviour

S: my friend

M: 'I want to get rid of you without you being aware of it'

Date: 8/12

No. 8

SS: My mother telling me that my father reacted negatively to the talk we had

R: I try to justify what I said by blaming him, but underneath it I feel guilty and I end up sending him a nice email

D: Primary Defence

SP: my mother saying about my father: 'He has to think about it, what you said really affected him deeply'

S: my father

M: 'You are no good'

Date: 9/12

No. 9

SS: my therapist tells me that he thinks that my wanting to record the session could stem from a desire to control

R: I try to explain why recording works well for me, but I feel insecure in doing so

D: Primary Defence

SP: his overpowering energy when he says this to me

S: my therapist

M: 'You have nothing to say here'

Date: 10/12

No. 10

SS: I look at my watch and realize I am going to be too late for my dental appointment

R: I say, 'Oh no, he's going to be upset'

D: Fear

SP: the dentist's angry face when I get there

S: the dentist

M: 'I don't want you around'

Summary of Phase 2: Finding the Sensory Perception and the Meaning

Please give yourself sufficient time to get skilled at finding the Sensory Perception and the Meaning. These are crucial steps in the PRI programme. In the beginning this may be something of a challenge:

- Remember to first go back in your mind's eye to the Symbolic Situation.

- Then find exactly that which you perceived *just before* your defence was activated: this is the Sensory Perception.

- Once you feel you are there, focus completely on the Sensory Perception, making it the sole focus of your perception. Imagine it coming closer and closer, getting clearer and clearer. Then ask yourself 'What message is coming at me through this Sensory Perception? What do I feel coming towards me from this Symbol?'

- Question yourself on the Meaning the perception has for *you*. Once you find the right answer you will know it, because you will experience an emotional reaction. Be it large or small, it will be there – *suddenly and sharply*.

Good luck – you can do it if you give yourself some time to train in this new skill. Be patient and compassionate with yourself. You are now consciously gaining access to your emotional brain.

Once you notice that you are able to find the Sensory Perception and the Meaning of most Symbolic Situations, you are ready to move on to Phase 3 – the last phase of this programme, the phase where the reprogramming starts.

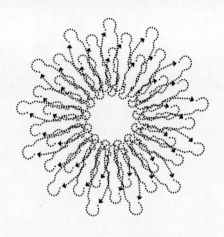

Phase 3
Defence Reversal:

How to Reprogramme Your Emotional Brain and Live Consciously in the NOW

Now I am
Free and connected
Loved
Without changing
How it was
I surrendered to the flow
And what overwhelmed and frightened me …
Appeared a dream
I became free
Of the illusion
To be how it was
VERA BOSCH, *COMPASSION*

After having gone through Phase 1 – self-observation leading to recognition of defences – and Phase 2 – understanding which Symbols activate your defence and dissecting the Symbols into each Sensory Perception and its Meaning – you are now ready to take the last step in this programme.

Please make sure that you have become skilled in the steps of Phases 1 and 2, however, before moving on to Phase 3. As I explained, each phase builds on the previous and, as PRI is a very precise instrument, *shortcuts don't work*.

One of my students once said, 'PRI is like doing maths with emotions, it is that exact.' And she was right. The defence 'programme' installed in our brain works like clockwork. In order to break its code we have to approach it with exactly the same precision. Either the code we enter is right and the lock opens, or the code is wrong and the lock doesn't move an inch. Put in other words: if the code is wrong, the emotional brain will not open itself to us so we can look at and work with what is hidden inside it.

Defence Reversal

So how do we reprogramme our emotional brain once we have gained access by recognizing the defence mechanism that has been activated (Phase 1), then finding the Symbol that brought this on and dissecting it into the Sensory Perception and its Meaning (Phase 2)?

The key is what is called Defence Reversal. Defence Reversal is a technique – again, as with everything else in PRI, it is not general but very precise – that will help us to get out of our defensive thoughts, behaviour or feelings. It will help you to access the old pain touched upon by the Symbol. Then you will find out for yourself that defences really do hide painful, yet old, experiences and that you don't have to defend against these in the present – old stuff is old; it's over and done with. What good news!

Stop Living in the Past

Every time we let ourselves be taken over by a defence and we buy into its message that 'Yes, there *is* a problem now,' we strengthen the grip which our outdated defence system has on our lives. In a way, this amounts to still living in the past instead of in the now.

What a shame and what a waste of your life, which could be so fulfilling. We get stuck all over, and over and over again, in believing and feeling that we are unloved, unwanted, not appreciated, not listened to, without meaning, or worse ... Having to live through this as small children was bad enough. To keep on recreating the nightmare again and again, long after it is OVER, is an even bigger tragedy. *You don't have to buy into it.*

Once you know the way the psychological immune system, as I like to call our defences, works, you can crack its code and deactivate the programme – the programme which has not only become outdated but is actually quite harmful to both your emotional and your physical wellbeing. Overeating, alcohol abuse, addictions, stress, anger, depression, fear and anxiety, to name just a few examples of defences, all have a direct influence on our physical wellbeing.

The Price We Pay for Living Defensively

Being fully aware of the price you pay for living defensively will motivate you to start applying these steps. Knowing that Fear and the Primary Defence spoil your life is obvious, but the price of False Hope, False Power and Denial of Needs may not be as clear. Unfortunately it is just as high.

Every time you let yourself slip into False Hope you are giving yourself the message that your life now is not giving you what you hope to get through the False Hope behaviour. For example, say you are hoping for appreciation by doing your utmost for your dinner guests. You are actually confirming your deep (old) feeling that you are not sufficiently appreciated now. In this way it is as if you are reactivating your old pain again and again. As a result, no matter how much appreciation you receive in the present reality, you will never be able to feel it as such.

False Power not only creates many conflicts in your life, but it works to convince yourself over and over again that you are being treated badly in the present.

As for Denial of Needs – apart from the emotional poverty you are condemning yourself to – it strengthens the idea that you need to distance yourself from all kinds of unpleasant things. In that way it becomes hard to discover that there may not be as many unpleasant situations as you tend to be convinced there are ...

What a high price we pay for our defences. And what do we get for that high price? Behaviour that is familiar to us and therefore seems to be 'safe', but which in fact is destructive and sabotages our lives.

The good news is that it doesn't have to stay that way.

WHAT YOU DO IN PHASE 3

Preliminary Steps

> The first step is to put into words a specific emotional problem you have in your life that you would like to do something about.

Be sure that the thing that you would like to change is defined as something specific. For example 'I don't want to feel unhappy' is *not* specific. Instead, try to link the feeling of unhappiness to specific situations in which you feel it most strongly. For example: 'When my husband is gone in the evening, I feel unhappy.' This doesn't mean that there aren't any other situations in which you feel unhappy, but for now you need to find one specific situation to apply PRI to. Once you have done that successfully, you can apply PRI to any other situation you want to change. But for now just find one specific situation in which you feel strongly the feeling you would like to change.

Once you have clearly defined the feeling by linking it to one specific situation in which you feel it really strongly, you can ask yourself if the emotion itself could be further specified. Maybe the general feeling of 'unhappiness' could be described more accurately as 'loneliness' or 'rejection' or 'insignificance'? The more exact you can be about the emotion you would like to do something about, the easier it will be to take the necessary steps.

Here are a few more examples to help you be precise.

Instead of	You could say
I often feel stressed.	When I run into John at work my heart starts racing and I become really anxious.
Nobody likes me, I am boring.	During the coffee break at work, I don't know what to say and I feel left out.
I hate it when the kids don't listen.	I start screaming when my children fuss in the morning and we start to run late.
I am always running around taking care of other people.	When my friend wants to see me I always go over, even if I am really tired.
I don't dare confront other people.	I am afraid to tell my brother that I don't want to spend Christmas with him.
I have a hard time when people nag me.	I get angry when my wife criticizes me.
Crowds scare me.	I get panicky when I am exposed to large groups of people I don't know.

I'm sure by now you've got the picture about how to be specific about your emotions!

Write down what you would like to change in your life. Then, if necessary, specify what you have written down by describing a concrete situation and maybe rephrasing the emotion as well, so that it describes what you feel as precisely as possible.

In order to give yourself a good chance to train your PRI skills, start out with something that presents itself quite often in your life. Preferably on a daily basis. This will give you ample opportunity to practise and learn.

Also, I advise you not to start out with a problem that is too big. Big issues like addiction or deciding whether to get a divorce or not are *not* a good starting point. Don't make it too hard on yourself right from the start. There will be more than enough opportunities for that later. Remember, once you learn how to work with this first problem, you will then be able to apply the PRI technique to other situations that you want to change.

Give yourself one week to come to a good choice of a first problem to work with.

Continue doing your self-observation, write down in your PRI notepad any defences you notice during the day, take a maximum of 15 minutes once a day to analyse one or more Symbolic Situations and break them down into Symbol, Sensory Perception, Meaning, Defensive Reaction and Defence Category. After a week you should have a good idea of which specific problem it is you want to work on first.

Then ask yourself which of the five defences is at the core of your problem. Is it that you're angry or irritated? If so, you will benefit from working with your False Power. If you are scared or anxious, then the work I suggest for the Fear defence will help you. Are you feeling mostly numb, cut off from your feelings? Take a look at what I advise for Denial of Needs. Or when you are feeling really low about yourself, insecure, depressed or guilty, then it is the Primary Defence that you need to focus on. Last but not least, if your problem is about stress or living mostly 'for others', then it is False Hope that has caught you in its web.

What exactly you can do to free yourself is what I will explain next.

Summary of the Preparatory Steps of Phase 3

1. *Continue doing your daily self-observation (notes all day and Self-observation Form 2 – Phase 2 once a day).*

2. *Describe a concrete situation and concrete emotion you want to work with.*

3. *Make sure it is something that occurs often.*

4. *To start out with, choose something that is not too big.*

5. *Take a week to choose the first problem situation you want to apply PRI to.*

6. *Then decipher which defence is at the core of the problem.*

You can now move on to step 2 of Phase 3.

Defence Reversal Technique

> Defence Reversal: saying 'no' to the tricks your mind is playing on you, surrendering to old pain and discovering the NOW.

First of all, put into words what your Defence Reversal might be. Once you know which defence is activated in the situation you would like to change in your life, you can determine which steps to take in order to deactivate the defence and reprogramme your emotional brain in the process.

This work is really exciting because you will start getting glimpses of the NOW, glimpses that will last longer and longer and become more and more frequent. Your emotional brain will not be activated so frequently any more; as you start diligently reversing your defences there will be fewer and fewer signals activating your defences.

When this first starts happening, my clients are just amazed:

'Is this really possible? I wasn't afraid any more when my boss yelled at me! Am I in Denial of Needs or is this what you mean by Adult Consciousness?'

'I can't believe how my feeling towards her shifted after I had reversed my False Power defence. It's almost as if I am looking at another person, even though I know *she* didn't change but *my* perception of her sure did!'

'I am amazed, I went to those job interviews and did not feel inferior because of my lack of advanced training once!'

'I can now really let him go, instead of being obsessed by his leaving me. I can see that our relationship had no basis in reality, but it's OK. I feel at peace with the reality and connected in a loving way to him at the same time.'

'I still see the same facts as I did before when I was taken hostage by my defence, but it doesn't really affect me any more. Instead of getting angry with her so often and feeling threatened, I can now really feel there is no threat to me. I am really OK with her following the path she feels she needs to follow.'

In other words, after a successful Defence Reversal you will have managed to free yourself from your defence by first gaining access to the old pain, which was hidden behind the defence. This process then miraculously either changes your perception of the present problem, and therefore the way you feel about it, or, if your perception has remained unchanged, which can happen, Defence Reversal will have strongly changed your emotional reaction to the perceived problem.

Believe me, every time you do it correctly, so that the process works, it feels like a miracle. No matter how many times you experience it, Defence Reversal remains an amazing and extremely liberating experience.

Once you are out of your defence, you will automatically be back in the NOW. Then you will find that you can open your heart once again, because you are reconnected to yourself and therefore automatically to others. Your partner, your family and friends. And, probably most important of all, think of what it could mean to your children, to their future ...

So what does this miraculous process entail?

It takes *discipline* – not just doing it sometimes when you feel like it, but applying the exact steps *every time* that you have managed to hunt down a defence.

And it takes *dedication* – really *admitting* to yourself that you are caught in the claws of a defence, instead of trying to 'sell' it to yourself and others as a perfectly normal, appropriate and adequate response to the present.

This is not easy, because we really are taken hostage by our defences, and that means that we *completely* believe in the illusion that they are adequate reactions to the present instead of outdated and destructive survival mechanisms pertaining to the distant past.

So arm yourself with dedication and discipline and let's go and confront those defences of yours. You will see that each defence can be reversed by following the specific steps that apply to it. But beware: *the reversal steps do differ slightly between the different defences*. Take care to first be sure which defence you are dealing with. Then look up that defence's specific reversal steps in this chapter.[1]

DEFENCE REVERSAL STEPS FOR FEAR[2]

1. *Ask yourself 'What is it that I am most afraid of happening?'*

   We are afraid of that which has already happened. This question will get you into your emotional brain and show you something about your old reality.

2. *Imagine it happening in your mind's eye.*

   This will help you to gain access to the old repressed childhood pain.

3. *Allow yourself to feel the feelings that this brings up in you - don't feel the fear itself!*

   Allowing yourself to feel this pain, knowing it is old and cannot hurt you any more, is the first part of reprogramming your emotional brain.

4. *Do whatever you were afraid of.*

   This is the next part of reprogramming your emotional brain. By doing what you were afraid of, you will find out by experience that no matter what happens it is not dangerous in the present. (*NB* Please note that of course these steps do not apply when you [or someone for whom you are responsible] are in actual danger. In that case you need to take appropriate action in the present to ensure your safety.)

5. *Examine your perception of the Symbol and the way you feel about it now.*

   This is the final and most important part of reprogramming your emotional brain. By consciously noting and feeling the shift in emotional charge, and also usually in your perception of the Symbol, you really drive the point home that the present is very different from the past. That the past *is* past, and that only when we are caught in the claws of a defence do we perceive the present as if it were the painful past which we needed to repress as small children. Take a moment to notice what happens, now that you are no longer acting out of the Fear defence.

If you still feel afraid after taking these five steps to reverse your Fear defence, you have taken a wrong turn somewhere. Start over again. If you follow the instructions precisely, you will see and feel the liberating effect.

Example of Fear Reversal

I am afraid to ask my neighbour for help.

1. *Ask yourself 'What is it that I am most afraid of happening?'*

   I am most afraid that he will react in a very annoyed and rather aggressive way.

2. *Imagine it happening in your mind's eye.*

   In my mind's eye I see his face and imagine his expression and angry words (exaggerate if that helps to get to the feeling).

3. *Allow yourself to feel the feelings that this brings up in you - don't feel the Fear itself!*

   I feel a surge of sadness and loneliness come up, *fully aware that this is the old pain* and that it can't harm me any longer.

4. *Do whatever you were afraid of.*

   I go and ask my neighbour for the help I need.

5. *Examine your perception of the Symbol and the way you feel about it now.*

   I realize that even though he reacts a little grumpily, this can be understood: he's old, lonely and quite unhappy.

I feel empathy for him and, instead of leaving right away as I usually do because my Fear defence has been activated, I hang about for a little chat.

DEFENCE REVERSAL STEPS FOR THE PRIMARY DEFENCE

1. *Find the Symbol that started the Primary Defence.*

   The Symbol can be found by first determining the last moment you still felt OK about yourself. Then closely examine what exactly it was that happened immediately afterwards.

2. *Find the Sensory Perception and its Meaning.*

   In your mind's eye, focus on the Sensory Perception and the Meaning – exaggerate if necessary.

3. *Feel what this brings up for you.*

   Allowing yourself to feel this pain, *knowing it is old* and cannot hurt you any more, is the first step in reprogramming your emotional brain.

4. *Act contrary to the way you would have from the Primary Defence.*

   This is the next part of reprogramming your emotional brain. By doing now what you really could not get yourself to do when you were still in the grip of the Primary Defence, you will find out by your own experience that it isn't as hard as it seemed before. It might not even be hard at all!

5. *Examine your perception of the Symbol and the way you feel about it now.*

This is the final and most important part of reprogramming your emotional brain. By consciously noting and feeling the shift in emotional charge, and also usually in your perception, you really drive the point home that the present is very different from the past. That the past *is* past, and that only when you are caught in the claws of a defence do you perceive the present as if it were the painful past you needed to repress as a small child. Take a moment to notice what happens now that you are no longer acting out of the Primary Defence.

The Primary Defence is something to be very alert for when you are uncovering old realities and accessing old pains, since it comes up quite often. If you don't recognize it as a defence, you will quite probably think – because it is so painful – that it is old pain and believe it is beneficial to your healing process to allow yourself to feel the pain and cry it out. But the Primary Defence, with all of its pain, is still just a defence, a defence against feeling what, for the child you were, was even more painful and difficult to face: that your needs were not and would never be met. Therefore, when feeling the pain of the Primary Defence itself, what happens is that instead of healing ourselves we are actually strengthening this defence.

If you still feel insecure, guilty or overwhelmed after taking these steps to reverse your Primary Defence, start over again. It means you took a wrong turn somewhere. If you follow the instructions precisely, you will see and feel the liberating effect.

Example of Primary Defence Reversal

My friend not doing what she had promised me she'd do, making me feel I'm a nuisance.

1. *Find the Symbol that started the Primary Defence.*

   Symbol: my friend

2. *Find the Sensory Perception and its Meaning*

   Sensory Perception: not getting emails from her about our project

   Meaning: I want to get rid of (this project with) you.

   In your mind's eye, focus on the Sensory Perception and the Meaning.

   I imagine my friend having really 'had it' with me – in my mind's eye an image comes up spontaneously (don't think it up!) where I see her looking at me in disgust, turning around and walking away, leaving me behind.

3. *Feel what this brings up in you*

   This brings up a deep pain in my chest/heart area, I can feel that a great sadness is touched and brings tears to my eyes. I allow these feelings to take the time and space they need, *fully aware that it is old pain*.

4. *Act contrary to the way you would have from the Primary Defence*

   When I was in my Primary Defence I felt like avoiding contact with my friend. Now I reach out to her by writing her an email asking if anything is bothering her about our project.

5. *Examine your perception of the Symbol and the way you feel about it now.*

I now see that she was maybe busy or worried about other matters, and that even if she did not feel like finishing up our mutual project, it would not be a devastating rejection to me. A pity, sure, but no more than that. After my Defence Reversal and the email I send her, she replies that she really enjoys doing our project and that she was happy to receive my email ...

DEFENCE REVERSAL STEPS FOR FALSE HOPE

1. *Stop the False Hope behaviour – don't do the opposite, just go into 'neutral'*

2. *Ask yourself: When I ... (the false Hope Defence behaviour), what am I hoping for?*

Imagine that no matter how hard you try or what you do, you will never, ever get what you hope for.

3. *Feel what this brings up for you.*

Allowing yourself to feel this pain, *knowing it is old* and cannot hurt you any more, is the first step in the reprogramming of your emotional brain.

4. *Examine your perception of the Symbol and the way you feel about it now.*

This is the next very important part of reprogramming your emotional brain. By consciously noting and feeling the shift in emotional charge, and usually in perception as well, you really drive the point home that the present is very different from the past. That the past *is* past and that only when you are caught in the claws of a defence do you perceive the present as if it were the painful past you needed to repress.

5. *Note what happens in the NOW when you don't engage in your habitual False Hope behaviour. Do the walls come tumbling down?*

This is the last part of reprogramming your emotional brain. By noticing that the walls do *not* come tumbling down when you don't do what you usually do for others out of your False Hope, you will learn through your own experience that the urgency you've felt has all been in your own mind and in no one else's! What a liberating discovery ...

If you still feel stressed by urgency, a drive for perfection, obsessed with and craving for something, caught up in pleasing others, etc. after taking these steps to reverse your False Hope, start over again. It means you took a wrong turn somewhere. If you follow the instructions precisely, you will see and feel the liberating effect.

Example of False Hope Reversal

I keep taking work home with me during the weekends. My family is objecting.

1. *Stop the False Hope behaviour*

Unless there is an immediate danger of missing a deadline or losing my job this coming Monday, I am not going to take home any work this weekend.

2. *Ask yourself: When I overwork like this, what am I hoping for?*

What I am hoping for by working so hard is my boss being really happy with me and appreciative of all the extra work I am doing for him.

Then imagine that no matter how hard you try or what you do, you will never, ever get what you hope for.

I imagine not ever having my boss really happy with me nor appreciative of all I do for him, not ever, no matter how hard I try or what I do.

3. *Feel what this brings up for you.*

This causes a strong pain in my stomach to well up. It feels like a great loneliness. I allow it to move upward in my body, finally reaching my eyes and coming out as sadness and tears, *all the while aware that it is old pain I'm feeling*.

4. *Examine your perception of the Symbol and the way you feel about it now.*

I now see that my boss is rather disinterested in me; whether I work hard or not, he doesn't pay much attention either way, but he does seem to be OK with my work. What a different perception and experience of the situation. It sure lifts the pressure off my shoulders to try to please him and work so hard.

5. *Note what happens in the NOW when you don't engage in your habitual False Hope behaviour. Do the walls come tumbling down?*

My boss never made one remark about me not bringing in extra work after the weekend. He seems to be rather oblivious to what I do or don't do. No disaster happened! On the contrary, my wife is really happy that I am less stressed and can spend more time doing what I enjoy, instead of working so much.

DEFENCE REVERSAL STEPS FOR FALSE POWER

1. *Stop the False Power behaviour – shift into 'neutral'*

2. *Focus on the Symbol and ask yourself: What irritates/ angers me most?*

3. *Ask yourself: How does it feel to be treated this way?*

4. *Feel the feelings that come up, while being fully aware it is old pain.*

Allowing yourself to feel this pain, knowing it is old and cannot hurt you any more, is the first step in reprogramming your emotional brain.

5. *Examine your perception of the Symbol and the way you feel about it now.*

This is the next very important part of reprogramming your emotional brain. By consciously noting and feeling the shift in emotional charge, often accompanied by a shift in perception, you really drive the point home that the present is very different from the past. That the past *is* past and that only when you are caught in the claws of a defence do you perceive the present as if it were the painful past you needed to repress as a small child.

6. *Note what happens in the NOW when you don't engage in your False Power behaviour. Are you left alone, exploited, victimized, treated horribly?*

This is the last part of reprogramming your emotional brain. By noticing that the walls do not come tumbling down if you don't react judgementally or aggressively out of False Power, you will find out by experience that the problem was in your own mind and no one else's! Again, what a liberating discovery ...

If you still feel angry, irritated, judgemental, etc. towards the Symbol after taking these steps to reverse your False Power, start over again. It means you took a wrong turn somewhere. Remember you want to set the Symbol free, let the Symbol off the hook (also see page 50) so that you can do your Defence Reversal work! This is really hard in the case of being caught up in the claws of False Power. Don't fool yourself by saying you're not so angry, or that you don't judge but only evaluate others, etc; these are just a bunch of excuses that won't get you anywhere! Please follow the reversal instructions precisely; you will see and feel the liberating effects.

Example of False Power Reversal

My husband's new hobby – playing pool – is getting on my nerves and I'm sure to let him know on every occasion that presents itself.

1. *Stop the False Power behaviour.*

   I stop making negative remarks about it, I also stop showing my disapproval non-verbally by giving him the cold shoulder, and I stop the judgemental thoughts in my head.

2. *Focus on the Symbol and ask yourself: What irritates/ angers me most?*

   What angers me most is the emotional importance this new hobby has taken on for him. It is as if playing pool is all that counts, more than me even.

3. *Ask yourself: How does it feel to be treated this way?*

   Focusing on the idea that something else counts more for him than I do immediately brings up a feeling of sorrow as if there is nothing to live for any more.

4. *Feel the feelings that come up, knowing they are old.*

   I stay with the feeling as long as it lasts, making full contact with the lost and lonely feeling that wells up out of my chest, *fully aware that it is old*.

5. *Examine your perception of the Symbol and the way you feel about it now.*

   After these feelings I see the joy on my husband's face and at the same time his pain caused by my continual rejection. I feel sorry for him and the way I've treated him. I am still important to him; more important still, I can feel his love. I find that I can open up to him again.

6. *Note what happens in the NOW when you don't engage in your habitual False Power behaviour.*

   Not engaging in my judgement made the old pain come up and opened me to the present. My husband still loves his new hobby, but I can now see that I was never at risk of losing him or his loving attention. What a relief. I don't know where the situation would have ended had I kept on defending myself against my old pain by continually rejecting him openly or more subtly.

DEFENCE REVERSAL STEPS FOR DENIAL OF NEEDS

1. *Look for the Symbol.*

   You can find the Symbol by looking at what was going on in the moments just before you distanced yourself either emotionally or physically.

2. *Focus your attention in your mind's eye on the Symbol.*

3. *Ask yourself: What is it that I do not want to deal with, what do I want to avoid?*

4. *Focus your attention on this aspect of the Symbolic Situation and feel what that brings up for you, knowing the feelings are old.*

Allowing yourself to feel this pain, knowing it is old and cannot hurt you any more, is the first step in the reprogramming of your emotional brain.

5. *Go back – either physically or emotionally – to the situation you went away from when you were in the grip of your Denial of Needs defence.*

This is the next part of reprogramming your emotional brain. By going towards what you were avoiding from your Denial of Needs defence, you will discover that there is no need to isolate yourself from your feelings and other people any more. Sometimes things in the present might be unpleasant but they can never get to the point where you could not survive if you didn't activate a defence … You are *not* that small, totally dependent little child any more.

6. *Examine your perception of the Symbol and the way you feel about it now.*

This is the final and most important part of reprogramming your emotional brain. By consciously noting and feeling the shift in emotional charge, which is usually accompanied by a shift in perception, you can really drive the point home that the present is very different from the past. That the past *is* past and that only when you are caught in the claws of a defence do you perceive the present as if it were the painful past you needed to repress.

Take a moment to notice what happens now that you are no longer acting out of Denial of Needs. If you still feel out of touch, distant, aloof, not so involved or uninterested, etc. after taking the six steps to reverse your Denial of Needs, start over again. It means you took a wrong turn somewhere.

It can be hard to recognize Denial of Needs, since it is characterized by a lack of feeling. Don't fool yourself by saying nothing's wrong, that there is nothing to worry about, that all is fine when in fact you feel emotionally flat. This kind of denial will not get you anywhere!

Please follow the reversal instructions precisely; you will see and feel the liberating effects.

Example of Denial of Needs Reversal

I don't tell my wife that I've lost my job. I convince myself that there is no hurry, it can wait, this will be better for her as well.

1. *Look for the Symbol.*

   My wife is the Symbol.

2. *Focus your attention in your mind's eye on the Symbol.*

   I see my wife in my mind's eye.

3. *Ask yourself: What is it that I do not want to deal with, what do I want to avoid?*

   I'm postponing telling her I lost my job so I can avoid her anger and her not wanting to have anything to do with me any more.

4. *Focus your attention on this aspect of the Symbolic Situation and feel what that brings up for you, knowing the feelings are old.*

I imagine that she gets very angry and throws me out of her life. This brings up a very uncomfortable feeling – it feels very threatening. I feel pain in my chest, knowing this is the old pain.

5. *Go back – either physically or emotionally – to the situation you went away from when you were in the grip of your Denial of Needs defence.*

I go up to my wife that evening, after the kids are in bed, and tell her I lost my job. It is hard to tell her. She is shocked by this news that she hadn't expected, and reacts with anger and irritation. She is worried about my career and our financial situation.

6. *Examine your perception of the Symbol and the way you feel about it now.*

I look at my wife and see her worries, which I can understand. I can feel compassion for her. It is obvious that underneath her anger she is hiding fear. Even though the situation and my wife's reaction are not pleasant, I can remain centred in the present and deal with the present-day situation, instead of avoiding it out of fear of my wife, like so many times before.

Beware: during reversal step 4 – feeling the pain that is being touched upon – that you really *feel* it is old pain, instead of just *knowing* this rationally. If you are not sure about this and think: 'Yes, but I feel it now, don't I, so how can I know it is old?' ask yourself the following four questions:

When I allow this feeling to come up, do I feel:

1. *small (the other person seems much bigger/stronger/ more powerful than me)?*

2. *vulnerable (the other person can do with/to me what he wants)?*

3. *dependent (I need the other person to fulfil my needs)?*

4. *without a sense of time (it seems as if the situation will always remain as it is now)?*

Or is what you are feeling the emotion of an independent adult who can take care of his own needs, knowing that everything has a beginning and an ending, that nothing is forever?

If you recognize yourself in the first four questions, then you can know and feel that what you are feeling is the old pain of the child you were. It is not the pain of an independent adult, the adult you have become in the meanwhile. If you are feeling old pain without emotionally realizing that it is old, you will strengthen the defensive illusion that it *is* happening now … beware.

I would like to give you one more example of how PRI helps us to unravel our emotions and live life to the fullest. In this situation you can see how this woman was able to take one PRI step after the other, smoothly and without difficulty. This example very well describes what becomes within our reach by doing PRI.

. . . .

I once had a telephone conversation with a dear friend of mine who has been struggling to break out of a relationship that was very intense and very hard for her to let go of. After she had once more talked to her ex-boyfriend, she told me in a disappointed and hurt sort of way that she didn't want to be in touch with him any more for a while. Obviously a defence had been activated. A few hours later she then wrote me an email:

> I got through it!!
>
> I felt such a deep urge: I am going to call him, I want to be in touch, I want him to stay with me ... False Hope. I then found Martin's exact words that touched me: 'You have to move to the spiritual level ... Nicole. What are you doing with yourself? I have to go to give a client a treatment now, I can feel that I am in a very high state of consciousness. I don't have any more time to talk to you.'
>
> The Meaning I gave to these words of his was: 'I reject you ... you're making a fuss and exaggerating.'
>
> Then suddenly I saw the old reality that was hidden in the present.
>
> I was sitting on a very small chair and was being left behind. The person who left me behind went on happily with his own life and didn't bother with me.
>
> I cried so hard.

Now I don't have to obsessively try to re-establish contact with Martin, and I also understand the False Power I was in yesterday. The stronger the defence, the stronger the pain. I know you helped me ...

Thank you!

Lots of love, Nicole

PS I am now going to temp agencies to look for a job!! And I know I will find one.

. . . .

Let's Do It

Now it is up to you.

1. *Look back at the problem that you wanted to work on.*

2. *Ask yourself which defence is involved.*

3. *Once you know which defence is involved, look up the specific reversal steps for this particular defence.*

4. *Then write out the first steps of the Defence Reversal and, when you think you have a pretty good idea of what you need to do, go and do it!*

⇨ *@ If you want you can download the Phase 3 form from the PRI website*

PRI Defense Reversal (DR) form – Phase 3

DR form	
Date:	
Problem that I want to work on:	
Defence involved:	
Steps for Defence Reversal:	
1.	
2.	
3.	
4.	
5.	
6.	
Date:	
What I did:	
And the direct effect:	
Date:	
Result after a while:	

Once you feel you have made enough progress with the first problem you chose to work on, you are on your way to tackling the next one. Just about anything now comes into your scope and power to change. It might need some practice at first, but if you apply yourself you will get the hang of it.

As you work your way through the PRI steps, you will see that it becomes a self-enforcing process: the more you do it, the better you get at it, the better the results will be and the more this will stimulate you to put more effort into working with your problems. Problems which, in the end, turn out to be nothing but your defences.

Unfortunately, the opposite holds true as well: the less you invest in this process, the fewer results you will get, the less you will be inclined to invest, etc. So be aware and choose which outcome you want to put in motion – it is your choice.

What a new way of looking at life, and what great possibilities this opens up for living life to the fullest. As it turns out it is *you* who creates your own reality, not your boss, not your wife, not your children, not your neighbour or anyone else. The good news is that this then makes it possible for you to unravel your emotions and take your emotional wellbeing into your own hands, instead of being dependent on anyone else as you were when you were a child.

The world is out there: full of people and possibilities.

Go out and live life – this great present that we all receive – to its fullest, and may the divine Spark that shines in your heart lead you on your way.

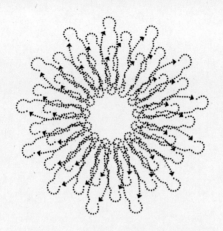

Case Histories

To inspire you and show you that PRI really works as well as I have described,[1] in this chapter I'll let others tell you their stories about PRI and what it has done for them.

Some of these stories have been written by people who have done PRI with the help of a PRI therapist. Even though many people do get good results applying PRI by themselves with the help of the PRI books, working with a therapist can be very helpful and, in some cases, even essential. This is especially true in instances of strong Denial of Needs defence (see for example Robert's story, page 94), where doing the work by yourself can be quite hard.

Also, the people who have been helped by therapists occasionally will make reference to the experience known as 'regression'. This technique for feeling old pain in depth is part of PRI therapy. In this book, however, as I have explained, the experience of getting in touch with old pain has been limited to accessing the old pain through dissecting Symbols and through Defence Reversal. In this book I wanted to present only the essentials of both the theory and method of PRI to you, to make PRI accessible to a larger public.

Please refer to my other books for more elaborate explanations of the PRI theory and method, if you feel an interest or a need to do so. Doing PRI 'self-help coaching' is possible as well. This is a specific and compact programme to help you apply the three phases of the method, either individually or in a group. Please see Appendix 6 for more about this.

. . . .

Robert
How I discovered that behind my 'perfect' life, Fear and Denial of Needs were stopping me from truly living

My life before PRI therapy was very steady. I actually thought I was perfect and I regarded people in therapy as losers. I had hardly any ups and downs. Often I wouldn't be able to know whether a situation was good for me or not. I didn't feel like there were any boundaries, so I often crossed them. The one thing I was struggling with was a constant sense of fear. Until the age of 35 I could easily ignore this. After that, the fear surfaced more persistently, which meant that sometimes I started to display avoidance behaviour. I actually had a 'good' life until my partner shook me awake with the words that she didn't know if she wanted to stay with me if I didn't show more of myself to her and didn't learn to deal with emotions. Driven by separation anxiety and False Hope I started PRI two years ago with a therapist.

My highest defence scores in the test prior to therapy were Denial of Needs and Fear. After the test I could make a start and I was instructed to write down all the situations where I felt negative emotions so that I could analyse them.

Oddly enough Denial of Needs was barely mentioned on the form, unlike Fear and False Power. The few times Denial of Needs came up on the form, I would talk about my trying to get out of tricky situations using lame excuses, such as: 'It wasn't meant like that' or 'It's no problem if I can't join them, because now I have time to read a book,' and so on.

I told my family about my strongest defence mechanism and asked them to point it out to me whenever they identified Denial of Needs. And indeed, I was 'fortunate' to have Denial of Needs and other defence mechanisms regularly pointed out to me. Without the feedback from my family, who could see my defence mechanisms better than I could, it would have taken me a lot longer.

After a while I recognized the feeling that goes with Denial of Needs: an empty calm. During meditation or when I am completely relaxed, I experience a full/abundant calm. From the moment I recognized the feeling and discovered that making lame excuses went with it, it was as if it were raining Denial of Needs the whole day.

Once I began to be able to deal with the Denial of Needs defence mechanism, I started to encounter more of the middle defence mechanisms: Primary Defence, False Power and False Hope. This was a turbulent time after a whole life of being emotionless. My life now felt like a tornado. It was hard work, every time I became defensive, to analyse and feel the situation and then reverse my defence mechanism. I noticed that all the situations that make me defensive are caused by the same old reality: as a small child I was given the message that I might as well not be here, I might as well be dead!

In the beginning, the analysis of one Symbol in terms of Sensory Perception and Meaning took me a quarter of an hour, in time this became only one or two seconds. Something that really helps me to recognize defence mechanisms, especially the difficult-to-identify defence mechanisms Denial of Needs and False Hope, is to check whether I still feel connected with the other person. If I don't feel like that, then I must be using a defence mechanism. After I have analysed the Symbol and reversed the defence mechanism, I look at the situation afresh in the light of the present and I am usually amazed at the new picture and feeling I then have. A picture without pain and with a clear feeling of connection to the other person. Unbelievable.

I have PRI to thank for the fact that I am now finally LIVING. I go through life relaxed most of the time, I relish the bond I feel with my children and partner, I enjoy better health, pleasant emotions, smells and colours, nature and starry skies. Everything is now clear and intense, even negative matters and events.

Looking back, I am very grateful to my partner. If she hadn't confronted me, I would have carried on forever with my life of Denial of Needs. What a dreadful shame ...

* *

Marianna
How I couldn't control myself and used to hit my son, even though I knew better... and what PRI has meant for me

The birth of my son Dave caused a huge crisis. Until then I thought I had it made: a good job, a nice husband, a nice house, etc.

Until then I had been able to organize everything as I wanted, but now Dave called for me at the most inconvenient moments and I 'had' to come to his rescue. In any other situation I would have been able to say no; in this case, however, that was impossible. His crying made my heart miss a beat. I developed a kind of panic reaction which meant I just *had* to comfort him. I had no more time for anything any more. Even the most basic things such as getting dressed and eating were impossible to do without interruption, without having to attend to Dave. For that is how it always felt: like I 'had' to. I was constantly torn between my needs and his.

When I was four months pregnant with my second child the strain was so great that I gave Dave a 'smack' for the first time. I write this in quotation marks because what we call smacking with regard to children would be called 'hitting' among adults, and of course that is exactly what it is. I had been angry with him before, but I managed to justify that to myself. I felt from the start, however, that hitting was wrong. I knew perfectly well that it was harmful to his emotional development and I could also see – unfortunately only after my anger had cooled – how bad it was for him.

In my search for a solution to my situation I read everything I could get my hands on about parenting, I took courses and fought against my impulse to hit him. After a while I conquered my embarrassment and plucked up the courage to mention it to a social worker. 'You shouldn't do that,' was the reply. After that I really didn't know where to turn. From conventional means to alternative assistance, parenting courses and Bach Flower remedies, nothing helped. And every day my husband returned home with the question: 'How did it go?' Most days to my great shame I had to admit that I had hit Dave at least once. Two times it went even further than 'mere' hitting. I can still vividly recall both times. Awful. That I actually did that.

That I, who wanted so badly to be a loving mother, time and again became a sort of monster who had no control over her emotions and assaulted her own child whom she loved so much …

And then one day, my husband brought home *Rediscovering the True Self*. I read it, devoured it and knew: 'This, this is what I can do.' I immediately started applying the PRI principles. It soon became crystal clear that my anger was a defence mechanism that was taking me hostage, as it were. I learned how to recognize when this was happening by becoming aware of the signals in my body when the anger approached: a sort of volcano which, so it seemed, just had to erupt. Next I learned how to stop this volcano: by looking at it, by stepping outside myself as it were: by feeling the anger raging through my body and knowing at the same time with my intellect that I didn't have to do anything, *I didn't have to go along with it.*

What exactly was it about Dave that made me so angry? That he got in my way, didn't cooperate, did exactly what he wanted, without considering me for even a second or what that meant for me. As if it didn't matter to him that I was tired, in pain, or needed a break. That was the illusion my False Power tried to feed me, I discovered later on. The Sensory Perception turned out to be Dave's crying when I was busy and the meaning that came to me at those moments was: 'Your sole reason for existing is to fulfil my needs.' By not giving in to my anger, but just looking at it, I gained space in which I could then ask myself what exactly 'made' me so angry.

I felt powerless, hopeless and worn out, without consolation, without anything at all 'for me' in the life I was leading. As a child I didn't get what I needed. In exactly the same way I was passing this on to Dave. It turned out that I, too, had been hit. I, too, had been confronted with my mother's despair, the anger and the bitterness and I, too, had also been let down by the person who should have done something about it, my father.

Applying PRI – confronting the Symbol, rather than constantly avoiding the difficult situation with the help of 'tips and tricks' from books and courses – has had an enormous effect: I hardly hit my son any more after that. I now had an instrument to work on my anger. I was no longer powerless, at the mercy of my defence mechanism and, step by step, with ups and downs, I could chip away at the False Power defence mechanism. I realized how little those terrible feelings had to do with Dave and therefore how little it all had to do with the here and now, with my present situation, with my present-day life as an adult. In this way I was able to develop compassion for myself and understand why I had hit him time and again.

The atmosphere in our family has been transformed, like I'd never dared hope it could be. We now have love and understanding and attention for each other. And this means that the children are also getting on with each other better and better, that my husband and I are much closer, that my work is going better and my social life is expanding. Since PRI, a path has opened up where before there was only a dead-end street. And if I keep following it, no matter how difficult and confrontational it sometimes might be – it really is vital to conquer the defence mechanisms, to have the discipline to recognize the defence mechanism and reverse it – every day I notice a lightness in my life that previously I could have never have imagined.

. . . . » » » »

Joan
How I beat my migraines by reversing my Fear defence mechanism

I used to suffer terribly from migraines. When I was working as a trainer I often had a migraine either before, during or immediately after a two-day training course. I would lie in a hotel room for a whole day, dead to the world, and a colleague had to take over. Apart from the terrible headache, an attack was always accompanied by nausea. For hours I would vomit every 10 to 15 minutes. In the last year I worked as a trainer this happened every week.

I knew that these attacks had something to do with the strain I was under and with the fact that I was scared. But I had no idea what I was scared of. In the end I quit giving training courses. I blamed those training courses, even though I knew perfectly well that I'd been suffering from these attacks since I was 18, and back then I obviously wasn't giving any training courses!

During my PRI process I started becoming better and better at paying attention to exactly when these attacks happened and what I was doing at the time and how I felt just before the attack started. I discovered that it had to do with situations I feared or dreaded and that I couldn't avoid in the short term.

Last year I was going on holiday with my daughter and her 18-month-old son. My daughter discussed it with a friend and this friend also wanted to come with us. However, this friend had just arranged to meet her in-laws, so she wanted to bring them along, too. My daughter asked if this was OK with me and I said, 'Why not?', while inside I felt like I'd rather go with just my daughter and grandson, but didn't dare say so. In this way I was suddenly on my way to Menorca with an extra three strangers – instead of just my daughter and grandson.

The days went by and increasingly I felt myself becoming a kind of alien in the group. I didn't know what to do. No one could see anything on the outside and on the last day the inevitable had come: a migraine attack. As usual, without me understanding why this was happening.

Now I know that in my case migraine attacks are all about the Fear defence mechanism. Before PRI I barely recognized this fear, wasn't really aware of it. I didn't even recognize the tension in my body, because it was so normal to me. I would always wait until the fear passed, and then just step right into another defence mechanism.

Thanks to PRI I recognize this fear a lot faster and a lot better, especially the physical aspects. When I identify it in time, I can reverse the fear and then I don't get a migraine! When I don't identify it and find myself in another defence mechanism (usually False Hope alternates with False Power), I reverse this defence mechanism and then I usually don't get a migraine either.

Sometimes I get a migraine anyway, which means that I have been led astray by defence mechanisms in the silent False Hope that it might actually work this time and I won't get a migraine. That is never the case. My first inclination, once I have a migraine, is to just sit it out passively. I try to keep myself as calm as possible and try to relax.

A little while ago I discovered that this behaviour of passively sitting it out and trying to relax was an attempt to make the migraine go away. It was therefore False Hope! This was a very important discovery. I realized that the migraine had thus become symbolic. When I reversed this False Hope, I experienced the migraine as a big black darkness completely overwhelming me, with no escape. I soon recognized this as my old reality. The reality of the small girl I used to be, whom nobody cared about. I was able to accept the old pain. After that there would be a true relaxation: the migraine faded away!

Recognizing defence mechanisms and reversing them has really helped cure me of my migraines. The attacks have been reduced to about once a year and then, even if I do get a migraine, I can make sure it doesn't last long.

For me this is nothing less than a miracle and I want the world to know about it. How often have I heard that migraines simply run in the family, that they are a physical problem and that I should just learn to live with them? I now know for sure that this is nonsense. I hope that other people take hope *and* inspiration from my story.

* *

James
How Denial of Needs was controlling my life and how PRI got me back in touch with my body and my family, and how, as an extra bonus, I lost 15kg without effort

I was struggling with fear and feeling desperate. I was 48 and did not feel good about myself. And I felt at risk of illnesses like diabetes, but I had no idea about how to change my (eating) habits by myself. Research I had participated in was clear: stop dieting and find a therapist. It turned out that there was a direct relationship between eating and my emotional state. In PRI words: Denial of Needs. Understanding this, stopping the behaviour and reversing the defence, feeling what my defence was protecting me from, has been a long and difficult process.

When I started with PRI, I thought: it is now or never. I had been trying to process my childhood for more than 25 years, and sometimes I believed I had succeeded. But I kept running into the same old irrational things, like anger attacks which, thanks to PRI, I understood were defences activated by a Symbolic Situation. Before I did PRI I used to think that those anger attacks were a result of my character and temperament. Also, I had been convincing myself that this behaviour was very advantageous for me. I have been in charge of very big and successful projects and everything I touched seemed to work out well. I looked mainly within myself for the cause of my problems, fear and desperation. I thought something was wrong with me.

When I read *Illusions* and *Innocent Prisoners*, I was at first very enthusiastic about the method. But further down the road it turned out to be more difficult than I had thought. Often I found myself waiting for 'it' to happen, and I was trying to apply PRI from a sort of cramp. And I was disappointed when it turned out that after getting rid of one defence I had just invited another one in. This was a long and enervating process, but the self-observations and finding the Symbol in the end gave me great results. PRI has won a place in my daily way of doing things, in my way of thinking. It is my antennae that let me know immediately: I am in a Symbolic Situation!

I have learned to face the fact that I was abused as a child. I was not allowed to think what I thought, feel what I felt, be what I was. I suffered from the judgement of God and people. The hardest thing for me in PRI was to disconnect the old pain from the present situation. In the beginning the defences still made me attach the old pain to the Symbol, in the Now, instead of being able to recognize it as an old feeling. I can now say that I have learned to feel old pain as old pain.

I have learned that Denial of Needs was and sometimes still is an important part of my adult life. Watching TV, (over)eating, working hard, always busy devising things and creating a hectic environment were its main characteristics. Denial of Needs was not easy to recognize, because it numbs feelings.

A lot of Symbols that I learned to recognize and analysed turned out to be linked to my feelings of dependency, in combination with threat and intimidation. I used to think that I knew my own life, after all I had always been a part of it, but in the past three years it has been a shock to discover how bad it really had got. The dependency and threats had been so all-encompassing that they had permeated my whole life, long after the end of my religious upbringing. Before I discovered PRI I thought that many things were 'normal'.

I have also learned what it means to be a 'knowing parent'. Bit by bit I've told my teenage daughters about PRI. I was sad to find out that they were scared of my False Power defence and of the desperation hidden behind my False Hope behaviour. A few times they pointed it out to me when I was 'too angry' and they have told me, 'You have become much more relaxed.' That's right, there is more peace in my life, in our family and we have a lot of fun.

An important mantra that I've picked up from the books and the sessions is: 'The past is over.' I remember shouting it out loud once during a walk in the woods: 'How fantastic that the past really is over!' It no longer has to be present as a heavy burden weighing on my shoulders, as a stone that I

---

keep bumping into every day. I don't have to mix the sadness, pain, loneliness and intimidation of my childhood with my life, my relationships and ambitions of the present. I am no longer at the mercy of my defences, but can recognize and reverse them. This is really an enormous liberation, which I am experiencing more and more with each day that passes.

And last but not least, without going on a diet I lost 15kg 'without any effort', after discovering that I was very often eating out of a defence. I had almost forgotten to mention my weight loss in this story, it happened that naturally. What a piece of luck!

Julia
How I went from feeling like a bottomless pit full of need for appreciation to a completely unexpected and all-fulfilling feeling of happiness

It had been quite a while that I had been struggling with the feeling 'Notice me and think of me as someone who matters.' I would do just about anything to be considered friendly, smart, interesting, clever and fun. I did my utmost to get appreciation from others. This in itself never seemed problematic to me, but it was continually present in the background and the appreciation was never enough. My need was a bottomless pit and made me feel dependent.

I started filling out the Self-observation Form. I discovered several defences: before my mother comes to visit me I start cleaning the house, for example, or I insist that my partner starts cooking earlier because otherwise the children will be in bed too late, or I really do my best to convince my therapist that I am working hard.

By observing my behaviour and analysing situations time and again, I learned how often I really was coming from a defence. In my case, mostly False Power and False Hope. It was so familiar to me to live in that way and I was used to the energy and atmosphere it created.

Until one Wednesday morning, a week after a very intense session with my therapist about reversing the Primary Defence. I was biking through the city with my 2-year-old son in his bike seat just in front of me. Suddenly the moment touched me deeply in my heart. I was overwhelmed by an enormous feeling of happiness that kept going on. At first it felt a bit strange, but it really overwhelmed me completely. It was so unexpected, and at the same time so all-fulfilling. This experience opened my eyes to how beautiful life really can be if you experience it for what it is, without defences.

That moment turned out to be a turning-point in my process. I learned to reverse the False Hope and the False Power and discovered that my way of looking at the reality could change completely within just one minute. It made me happy, I was able to stay in touch with myself and to fully enjoy the here and now.

It turned out that my defences stemmed from an old unfulfilled need: 'Take me along, hold me and cherish me.' Realizing that this had not happened when I was a young child, smacked me in the face.

Allowing the old pain to come up was the next step in my process and gave me more space physically. By crying all those pent-up tears and feeling the pain that had been hidden deep inside, I was able to feel that I really didn't need defences against it any more. I have survived the painful past, I am here now, and I can let it go. No matter how hard I try, the longing that I had then: 'Notice me and consider me as someone that matters', shall never be fulfilled, nor will the reality that others let me down and left me ever change. Nor is that necessary.

Realizing that this situation once was life-threatening, but that I can now simply look back on it, helped me to allow the pain to come up and it diminished my fear. I was able to feel my great pain and show the world. I was able to let it out!

I have more peace, time and energy. I have more time for everything and I feel calmer at the same time. I never expected PRI to have so many side-effects, the most important being the deep feeling of happiness and the ability to profoundly enjoy the moment NOW.

PRI now asks continual watchfulness. I regularly find myself in a defence, but I am able to reverse it and can smile at it. Of course, in very difficult situations sometimes there still is a tenacious Primary Defence hanging around for a few days. But as soon as I really become aware of it and reverse it, the feeling of happiness returns. And that is something I never again want to lose ...

Joy
How my relationship improved when I worked on my False Power

For years I had been engaged in personal development and had already followed a large number of paths. I was driven by a frequent inner sense of emptiness and stress, and I often felt angry with other people. In particular I was very often irritated by my husband, even though I loved him a lot and really wanted to be with him. The sense of emptiness had also become a major part of my relationship with him. I often felt alone, abandoned. As a matter of fact I also had these same feelings at work and in friendships, but to a lesser degree. I knew that this was mainly to do with myself, but my idea of what might be causing this constant stream of anger and emptiness was simply too vague. In a few instances my quest had given me temporary relief, but mostly it had not given me much at all.

Through PRI I immediately recognized what was going on. All kinds of situations in the Now were connected with my past, without me being aware of exactly how this worked. I had known all along about the existence of defence mechanisms. But the precise way my consciousness and attention were captured by the operation of a Symbol was a complete eye-opener for me. It turned out that my emotional brain, filled with suppressed experiences from a distant past, was increasingly taking over from my rational brain, and what's more, without me realizing it. I recognized that this in particular was one of my biggest problems, because somehow I did know that in fact there wasn't a single missing ingredient in my present life.

In my quest I had long ago discovered that I could try to change or achieve all sorts of things, but this would not – or only temporarily – change my feelings of emptiness and unhappiness. Worse still, I'd been carrying on like this until the age of 40.

By means of self-analysis based on the PRI self-observation method, I discovered that Symbols related to my husband were operating in connection to the smallest things, things that would make anyone, any friend say: 'You're absolutely right, it *is* bad that he doesn't come home when he says he will, never calls, doesn't listen, doesn't …' A limitless array of behaviours. And all these things always turned out to activate my defence mechanisms.

What was actually happening was that I'd always react as if his behaviour were the end of the world: 'He doesn't love me,' 'He doesn't want me.' As if I were a young girl who simply couldn't live if he didn't do exactly as I wished. A wish that I began to recognize increasingly clearly as an old need that could no longer be fulfilled in the present.

By now I had also grasped that this insight alone was not enough, because the defence mechanism just carried on as before. The defence mechanism couldn't be beaten with brainpower alone. Indeed, I'd already been trying to 'think things away' for quite a few years. Through PRI I learned to recognize exactly what was affecting me in the Symbol of my husband. This turned out to be the speed and quantity of words I felt bombarded with. No harm done, you might think, but for me personally this torrent of words meant: 'I'll talk and you'll shut up. What you want to say means nothing to me.' As a result I found out that it was precisely this Meaning I felt when he spoke that was triggering intense False Power, and that this therefore had to be connected with old pain inside me. Once I realized this, I was able to start reversing the defence mechanism and keep feeling the old pain, knowing all the while it had nothing to do with my husband. Luckily I did realize this clearly: that a very important starting point in PRI is that you let the Symbol 'off the hook', by letting it go out freely. It had nothing to do with him, I would tell myself. In this way I could more and more often and easily overcome my own feelings of irritation towards him and avoid an argument, for example. It wasn't about him, after all. Even though he speaks fast, there wasn't really anything wrong with that, was there? And, does he really talk that much? In this way, the more I reversed my defence mechanism, the more I truly began to discover that the irritation defence mechanism was an inappropriate reaction.

What a relief this almost daily example alone gave me, him and our whole family. By constantly scrutinizing the False Power and other defence mechanisms, we now have a close relationship. It's not all plain sailing, but we always pull through. Especially because my husband has also started PRI himself, which has reduced the defence mechanisms in our relationship both on my part and on his. What a difference and what enormous possibilities!

* *

Irene
How my burnout turned out to be hiding a fear of failure and how I managed to free myself permanently from both

It all started when I broke down at work. Full of anger, indescribable anger, I entered the office of my company's social worker, who advised me to go and see the company doctor. After listening to me for a while, he asked me why I didn't 'just' stop being angry, so that I could find the rest I needed to recover. Something in me broke at that moment. Crying out loud, I told him that I wasn't able to do that because that would leave me at the mercy of the enormous fear I had carried inside for years. That was unthinkable, because after all I had given my all to overcoming that fear, desperately I had done everything in my power because I did not want to be the loser that I was so afraid of being. Since I was 20 I had been struggling through all sorts of therapies, awareness trainings, working on self-esteem classes, overcoming fear programmes, etc., etc. 'I have been there,' I said, and I thought 'not again with psychoanalysis'. I had already uncovered and analysed my childhood; enough was enough.

Someone familiar with PRI will recognize all five defences in this story. The False Power, the Fear, the False Hope, the Primary Defence and, not to forget, the Denial of Needs. A chain of different emotional states playing a game of ping-pong.

First of all I had to dive deeper into the theory. I read the books, reread the books, looked into them again. I started to get better at recognizing Symbols and defences, which made it possible to embed this knowing into my everyday life. I then started to practise, recognize and write down what kinds of situation I found myself in. Was I reacting from my Childhood Consciousness or was I able to act from the unburdened state of Adult Consciousness? What was the Symbol, what was the sting and which old pain was I denying? After that I made a start with opening up to the Old Pain. Pain that had been repressed so deeply that only my subconscious and my body were still 'aware' of it.

Before going any further I had to learn how to take responsibility for my actions. From there I had to become more and more aware of the how and why of my reactions. It didn't take me long to realize that I needed to get to work if I wanted to live a more unburdened life.

I started to work on my fear of expressing myself – either through writing or talking. I was always looking for the right word (False Hope), afraid that I wouldn't find it (Fear), sinking into an inferiority complex (Primary Defence), coming out of that filled with anger (False Power), in order to build a wall of indifference around me in the end (Denial of Needs). Pfffff. What an intense emotional struggle, and what a lot of pain and sadness. Well, I was ready to get rid of all that after 20 years!

Practising Defence Reversal during important meetings, conversations and conferences kept giving me more and more moments of being and acting unburdened. This then enabled me to see more clearly what was really going on, and to notice that during those moments when I was coming from Adult Consciousness I was able to be very to the point and that one of my strengths actually is to write down what I have to say. At those times I actually am a good guide for my subordinates, colleagues and even for my boss. But most of all I see how the change has affected the relationship with my husband and child. Especially my child reacts strongly, fully unconsciously and naturally to my diminishing defences. My biggest reward for all my struggling is seeing my child's increasing self-confidence in her daily life because of my different attitude towards life.

I have surfaced out of a really deep Primary Defence, in which I had the illusion that I was dyslexic, a bad mother, a partner not able to reach her mate and a boss who could not protect her subordinates. Is this what is called depressed?

My god, what deep pain and sorrow did that little girl have, what a big not understood world, what minimization of the suffering that is so often unconsciously inflicted on children. And what a relief once I was able to access the dramatic moment, to truly feel it for the first time and know where it belongs. It was as if a brick fell off of me, as if I never again would be taken hostage by that horrible experience. The link with the present had been broken. What a liberation.

But I already knew a lot about my childhood, didn't I? Yes I did, but only with my head. Now I 'know' it with my belly and especially with my heart. I am getting better and better at looking back on that old pain with compassion, leaving it where it belongs, in the past. I am on the right path.

. . . .

Felice
How fear that something would happen to my children was ruining my and my children's lives

After my eldest daughter was born, something happened to me. From the moment I looked this beautiful, vulnerable little creature in her sweet little eyes, I became worried. What if she weren't here any more? was one of my first thoughts. I couldn't bear those thoughts. At that moment a fear crept into me that would remain for years, albeit in varying degrees. I suppressed my fearful feelings and controlled my anxiety with the thought that any 'good' mother would be afraid to lose her child.

This fear manifested itself in various guises, from fear of cot death when my now two children were babies, to fear of all kinds of situations where something might happen to them and I wouldn't be able to protect, save or comfort them. For example, when other parents drove them places, when they did things and there was nothing else I could do to protect them. The number and kind of situations that I was afraid of was never-ending. My son's riding lessons, for examples, were pure hell. I was petrified that he'd have an accident. Purely to compensate I made one morbid joke about horses after the other. With this I kept my fear to myself as much as possible, but my children were well aware of it and this affected them quite a lot.

Meanwhile I had become a master at keeping an eye on their lives and telling myself that all parents are afraid. I disqualified parents who weren't afraid with the thought that they were bad parents. What's more, these fears were masked because I was not at all worried about myself. I was usually very fearless.

When my daughter was about ten, she wanted to start cycling, alone. Preferably to school on her own. I was at my wits' end. I came up with just about everything to postpone this inevitable event. Arguments such as 'you're too young,' 'it's still too dark outside, the street lighting is not so good and the weather is bad,' became increasingly untenable. She wasn't the type of child to let anybody stop her, I'd discovered long ago. In short, when it was no longer dark in the mornings, off she went. All by herself. With countless warnings and a new mobile phone in her pocket, she set off. 'Text me when you get there,' I cried.

I spent many days watching the clock. Often she didn't text me. 'Stay calm,' I said to myself at those times. 'She must have forgotten, don't bother her. She must have arrived ages ago and if not I'd have heard about it by now.' But that's precisely what I didn't manage to do. I'd ring her anyway, to check if she'd got there. So this is what I did every day, morning and night. 'I do trust you,' I'd say to her, as a sort of salve for her wounds, 'but I don't trust those tough cars.'

There was no getting round it now. I was totally ruining something that could have been nice for my children with my horrible fears. My son stopped horse-riding after a year and was inclined to be anxious. Fortunately my daughter carried on stubbornly and cheerfully cycling and I finally realized that I couldn't continue like this. I got in touch with a PRI therapist. The fear was too great to work on it alone. After reading the books, I no longer had to deny that being scared was an inappropriate reaction and I could acknowledge that my reaction was a fear defence mechanism.

What I couldn't stop myself from doing was justifying my anxiety. The therapist helped me to understand that I believed in three illusions. The first illusion was that I thought it was normal, even good, for me as a mother to be so anxious and that other 'good' mothers were also like that. The second illusion was the idea that I could always protect my children if only I were nearby to look after them. Even if I were to lose them, I needed to be close so they could die in my arms, in this way at least I would be able to comfort them. This also explained my lack of fear when we did things together, sustaining my illusion of control if only I were present. For example when it was me behind the wheel. The third illusion was that if only I gave very well-meaning advice and instructions, then nothing bad could happen. This stops children from developing self-confidence.

I started to work on these three illusions. Every single time that fear arose, I learned to stop it, as well as the cognitive illusions and misconceptions and also my behaviour. No more warnings, no mention of the rain, poor visibility or whatever. And then I learned to allow the old pain to come up. Again and again. It was quite a job, but I noticed that the fear did indeed diminish. My compulsive thoughts and the nervous clock-watching and staring out of the window decreased.

Later I found that my fear actually stemmed from a deep sense of abandonment, that my parents sometimes forgot about me when I was very young. That they paid me very little attention at all when I needed it so much, being just a small child. Very, very sad. Suddenly I also understood why I couldn't help thinking about my children so much and being so anxious. Incredible as it may be, it had nothing to do with my own children. Unconsciously my emotional brain was controlling me, that part of my brain full of awful experiences. Because of this, unintentionally but also unnecessarily, I really had stopped them from living and enjoying life to the full. From having confidence.

After a few months of PRI, including only a few weeks of reversing anger, I discovered one morning that I'd 'forgotten' to be afraid. My daughter had just received a new bike for her birthday. As it was green, we called it the Grasshopper, entirely appropriate for her. The sun shone on her beautiful long curls, her face to the wind as always. I waved, relishing the moment.

The fear hasn't disappeared completely. When my son wanted to start cycling two years later, it resurfaced very briefly. But by immediately reversing the fear defence it was gone in a few days. Very occasionally it reoccurs briefly in new situations. Yesterday I waved goodbye to my daughter the first time she took the train to a city far away. Now 14 years old, phone in hand, but now so that she can call her friends. I briefly felt the fear, 'She's going without me. What if ...?' Anybody would have called it an emotional moment between mother and daughter when I wiped away my tears, but by now I knew better and allowed my old pain to come up. She waved. She was bound to be a bit nervous about her first journey alone. But she was really looking forward to it. I waved back and texted her when the train was out of sight: 'Have fun, sweetheart!' Thinking: I am giving you to Life.

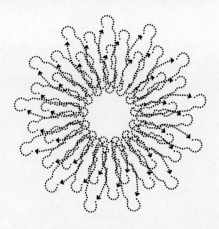

The Art of Conscious Living

Light the flame in your heart
Of love and truth forever
Close your eyes
And then make a search deep within,
Spreading the brightness of this flame.
With this flame, which is lit eternally,
Say my name[1]

SEEMA DEWAN, *SAI DARSHAN*

What, in the end, can come out of this Art of Conscious Living when applying the tools of PRI? The previous chapter showed you examples of the range of problems that PRI can be of help with. Now, at the end of this book, I would like to give you a little look at the way in which people start to experience life when they start passing more and more time in Adult Consciousness and less and less time in their defences. In other words, I would like to conclude by writing about the Art of Conscious Living, which seems to follow naturally out of doing PRI.

CONNECTION

One of the most important results of PRI is that people start to feel truly connected to others. During their PRI work they often begin experiencing feelings of fundamental connection to others, instead of feeling like a rather insignificant, isolated and, in the end, lonely individual being or 'mere body'.

In the beginning this feeling of connection will manifest itself especially with regard to loved ones, friends and family. Over time, however, the feeling can grow into a palpable sense of unity with all of creation. It might start extending to people we do not know, even to people we do not like so much, as well as to animals, to Nature and, finally, to all of creation around us.

The general sense is that a movement takes place from being small, insignificant and fundamentally alone to being an inextricable part of an immense Unity of connected expressions of Life. All space and matter, whether inanimate (for example a stone) or animate (a person, animal or plant) can be and are then seen as being permeated by the same cosmic life-force and consciousness.

A JOURNEY FROM THE SMALL 'i' TO THE 'WE'

From experiences such as these, where people lose their sense of fundamental separateness and move towards feeling part of a larger whole, we can truly wonder if life is not meant to be a journey from the small 'i' to the 'We'. From the ego 'I' to the Divine, united consciousness, where All is One.

If this is the journey that we are all on, with perhaps some people a little bit further along the way than others but all unmistakably travelling towards the same Goal, then what is the fuel that helps to propel us towards our final destination?

The best fuel, the fuel we all – with no exceptions – thrive on and which helps us move forward is, of course love and compassion. It's not success, not money, not good looks nor intelligence, not power, not control, not freedom to do what we want, not a trip around the world, not even a relationship, it isn't anything but the ability to love and give compassion that makes us thrive in the short *and* in the long run. Love for all beings, compassion for all beings.

Isn't love and its sister, compassion, what we all live for? 'All you need is love.' 'What the world needs now, is love sweet love.' 'Isn't she lovely, made of love?' Isn't almost every work of art about love? No matter how times change, love is always on our mind, whether it is foremost in our mind or present as an unconscious drive behind all we do. Without love babies wither away, without love life becomes bleak and meaningless, without love our hearts dry up, without love the little 'i' is all we have ...

So how do real love (not old unmet needs of the child we were) and real compassion (not False Hope) enter our lives?

The general interest in spirituality has been booming in the last two decades. When I was a student in the 1980s I remember that spirituality was not a hot topic. Students seemed to be mostly interested in political discussions: left- versus right-wing ideas against the background of the Cold War which had only recently ended.

This changed in the early nineties when a surge of spiritual revival seemed to be taking place: the so-called New Age was alive and kicking. New Age workshops became popular, as well as ideas about universal energy, healing, group hugs, swimming with dolphins and whales, and the Celestine Prophecy, to name just a few. The people engaging in these kinds of activity at that time, however, were still considered 'alternative'.

Now, almost 20 years later, spirituality seems to have made it all the way through to a large public. Eckhart Tolle's books are being embraced by Oprah, *The Secret* has sold millions of copies, meditation is widely practised and embraced by the scientific community, and, just like yoga, Tai Chi is becoming as common as aerobics was in the 1980s.

As you will have gathered, the spiritual path is important to me. In fact, it has been essential to me ever since I discovered Krishnamurti 35 years ago. The spiritual dimension of life has greatly touched my heart and I can only conclude that, in the end, life is about living from the Heart guided along by sacrifice, surrender and gratitude – or devotion, which is gratitude's 'exponential' form. Let me try to explain what I mean by these words.

SACRIFICE, SURRENDER, GRATITUDE

Sacrifice is about letting go of the ego. Instead of wanting certain things for our small ego-selves, being driven by desires and wanting to feel special and better than others, we can 'cut clear across the I'. To me this is the true meaning of the cross: the 'I' has been cut clearly across. It means that when we sacrifice our ego, we open our heart and live Life from a bigger perspective, a perspective where we can see all beings ultimately connected as one great expression of the Divine energy that pervades everything in our universe.

Looking at life like this is not something that we can decide to do rationally, at least not for most people. For most of us this will entail a long process of falling down and getting up again, hopefully learning the lesson, falling again and getting up again once more, etc., slowly moving towards a way of living that encompasses more and more love and compassion for *all* beings.

To those who have had a Christian upbringing, the word 'sacrifice' might be a negative, guilt-laden word. To those readers I would say that sacrifice actually can be joyous, once we give up our identification with the little 'i'. Once we start yearning to discover the 'We', sacrificing the so-called pleasures of the little 'i' – or perhaps, rather, dependencies due to 'slavery to the senses' – sacrifice actually takes on a very inspiring quality.

The five defences as I describe them in PRI offer a concrete definition of the ego, a word used widely in the spiritual lexicon. Every time we are trapped by one of the five defences we are imprisoned in our little sense of me, or ego. We are operating in a survival mode, our hearts necessarily closed. This means, for example, that we cannot truly see others for who they are and our struggle for survival will tempt us towards some pretty ugly thoughts, feelings or actions. Revenge, judgement, dishonesty, aggression, neglect, jealousy, hatred, egoism, betrayal, indifference, etc. are just a few examples of defences and of expressions of our ego and a heart that is closed.

Even seemingly nice behaviours might be nothing but unrecognized defences or ways for our ego to get what it wants: recognition, attention, sex, money, power, status, etc. Being nice does not always mean we are truly concerned for the person we are being nice to. It could very well be just about our own ego. Our 'niceness' merely serves as a way to get security, attention, friends, influence, money, etc.

'What's in it for me?' is the question the ego will put first. We might be so used to this that we are not even aware of it any more. We might think that we really are a 'nice gal' or a 'good guy', but ask yourself whom you are really concerned about in the end? Is it the other person or are you just using the other person for your own 'wellbeing' in the guise of friendship or love?

Sacrifice is about letting go of your defences. Truly admitting them and reversing them. Saying 'I am sorry' to your husband if you have been unfriendly to him, also (or especially) if he was giving you the cold shoulder first … Sacrifice your ego on the altar of Life: cut clear across the 'I'.

After diligently sacrificing our ego, reversing our defences in PRI language, we can start to see beyond our small self. Beyond our so-called needs and wants, our desires and defences. This will make it possible for us to start opening up to the experience that what life gives us will be exactly what we need in order to grow, even if it might be painful in the short run. Here we are entering the field of surrender. Surrendering to life, because we can trust that it is right: the little 'i' is not in the way so much any more, filling our heads with opinions and judgements, desires and ideas that are fundamentally alienating us from the bigger picture, from the 'We' perspective.

Surrender is about welcoming *all* of life's experiences and learning the lessons that are to be learned from these experiences. *Everything* becomes a gift when we can look at it in this way: something to learn a valuable lesson from, instead of something to resist, judge and reject. Something to welcome and go through, instead of something to fight against, to avoid or to flee from: 'What does this teach me?', 'How can I grow in this situation?' will then become key questions, instead of living from the basic 'like – attract' and 'dislike – reject' survival principle.

When we live from this basic survival principle we are completely guided by – I would rather say enslaved by – our likes and dislikes. If I like something, I want to attract it, hold on to it, do it again, not lose it; when I dislike something I will want to reject it, get rid of it, move away from it, get it out of my life. In this way it is easy to get stuck running after situations that will not teach us any valuable lessons, and avoiding those situations that would actually help us to grow as human beings on the path from the little 'i' to the 'We'.

In short, surrender is not about running after your likes or avoiding your dislikes. It is about welcoming *everything* on your path as a present because it is something that, if you allow it, can teach you a valuable lesson. I might try to resist conflict, illness and loss as experiences I do not want to have, but I can also choose to surrender and learn. Of course, our pain and suffering can be enormous. Nevertheless, we do have a choice between staying stuck in our suffering or feeling the pain and learning whatever there is to be learned from it.

Looked at this way, the biggest crises will turn out to be the greatest opportunities for growth. Isn't it interesting that the meaning of the word 'crisis' in its original Greek is 'opportunity/chance'?

Finally, from sacrifice of the ego and surrender to Life will come a deeply felt sense of gratitude. Gratitude for everything that comes our way will inspire us to become truly aware that the present is a present.

Gratitude and its exponential force, devotion, are not easy to describe or explain. Deeply felt gratitude towards Life, and devotion, are feelings and experiences that go far beyond the rational mind and that which words can describe.

While not being aimed at a Divine principle, and quite different in general nature, being in love is a feeling that mystics have said has the same intensity as the feeling of heartfelt gratitude towards Life, or devotion. However, being in love involves possessiveness, yearning for exclusivity, as well as lust – and it comes to an end. Looked at more closely, we could say that being in love is to a large extent about the illusion that we are getting our childhood needs met by the person we are in love with. Unfortunately, as we all know, this elating experience sooner or later ends, leaving us looking at the other person as someone with good and bad qualities, just like ourselves.

At that moment, *if we learn the lesson*, we face the conclusion that we will only find happiness in our own hearts. If we don't learn the lesson we will keep on looking outside ourselves forever, either trying to change our current partner, resisting accepting him or her completely, or looking for yet a new partner, only to come to the conclusion one day that we are again facing the same problems as before. The lover might be different, but as long as *we* don't change, Life will mirror back to us just that: our unchanged self with the same problems, hang-ups and illusions!

Gratitude towards Life and devotion, on the other hand,

are experiences which, once ignited, only grow stronger and stronger and can set our whole internal being ablaze. What ignites them is hard to know. Mystics and philosophers of all ages have pondered this question and not come to a clear answer. They do seem to agree that it is not something that you can deliberately go out and search for. Some search a lifetime and do not find anything, while others who are not even looking can be struck as if by lightning with a spiritual or mystical experience that profoundly touches their deepest being, leaving unmistakable and profound marks in the heart forever.

This can happen when you have opened your heart to a certain extent after working eagerly at crucifying your ego and surrendering to life. You are then in a more susceptible state to have the divine Spark within your heart ignite. At a certain point this Spark will stop quietly smouldering; it might light up fiercely and ignite your inner being. The more open your heart becomes, the more oxygen will be able to come in, setting you on fire internally, so to speak!

This is what is called devotion and is talked about in every mystic tradition. How well the Sufi philosopher and poet Rumi has put these feelings into words in his famous Rubais – a specific verse form in which he pours out his love for the Divine. I started this book with an example of one of his Rubais.

Sacrifice, surrender and gratitude, potentially developing into devotion, all lead to opening the heart and, in turn, are powered by an open heart, creating a self-reinforcing circle, leading to yet more willingness to sacrifice, more ability to surrender and a yet stronger experience of gratitude and devotion, on and on.

In the opposite direction the same movement can be seen. When we hold on to our defences and our ego, fight against the circumstances and experiences that Life brings us and fail to acknowledge the existence of a divine Spark, truly living from the heart can be quite a difficult endeavour. The sun may be shining outside, but if we stay inside with the shutters closed, we will never see the light nor feel its warmth. Even sadder, we can easily go on convincing ourselves and others that there is no such thing as a sun or light and warmth, and not even bother to go outside and take a chance ... So-called negative experiences will be perceived as threats to be bitterly fought against, the need to defend what I think is mine will only increase, feeling I could easily lose out, and my heart will close down more and more.

The choice is ours!

In the end, this is exactly what PRI is about. True surrender and deep gratitude become possible when we sacrifice our small 'i'. Once we move from sacrifice to surrender and finally to a deeply felt gratitude, love and compassion will automatically enter into our lives more and more. They are, if you like, the 'by-products' of living life from sacrifice, surrender and gratitude. Forever setting in motion our life's journey from the small 'i' to the Divine 'We'.

> Sacrifice the ego, so that you can surrender
> to Life with gratitude,
> and journey from 'i' to 'We',
> fuelled by love and compassion for all beings,
> every step along the way

A STAIRCASE TO THE ROOFTOP

It has taken me some time to come up with a good metaphor to describe PRI with regard to overall spiritual development. The most correct in my eyes is the metaphor of a staircase, not to heaven but to a more mundane rooftop.

PRI can be seen as a staircase starting in the cellar. In this cellar there is no light, it is dirty and there might well be a skeleton or two hidden in the cupboard. Before walking up the stairs, the cellar needs to cleaned and the skeletons hauled out of their hiding places. I am referring to the old pain and old reality that we have been hiding in our emotional brain since childhood. If we don't clean out our cellar, our emotional brain will keep on sounding the alarm every time something resembles the painful old reality we had to live through as children and we will be stuck or drawn back forever into the cellar of our life. With some beers and the TV maybe, but nevertheless confined in the dark without sunlight or a view.

Once this basic cleaning work has been done we can move on to the first floor. Here we see a few windows and the first light coming through. What a change: we can even look outside and get some idea of the great wide world that is out there and all the possibilities it might hold. If we continue with our PRI work, diligently observing and reversing our defences, the PRI staircase will take us up to the next level in the house, where the windows can let in more light and give us a better view than on the ground level. We are starting to feel that there is a lot more to be discovered outside the walls of our house. However, we still have a limited view since we are looking through window frames. We see parts of the larger reality, but other parts are still hidden from view. These parts that are still hidden represent metaphorically those parts of reality that we cannot yet see clearly because our defences are still distorting our perception without us being aware of it.

Continuing with the daily discipline of the PRI defence-hunt, we finally arrive on the rooftop. Once we have reached this stage we can look around freely in every direction and discover for ourselves what kind of world we find out there. What is there to be found is something for everybody to discover for themselves; no one can describe the light of sunrise to a person who has known only the darkness of night.

The rooftop is a metaphor for our Adult Consciousness: the aim of our PRI work. There we will see the present for what it truly is: surprisingly unburdened and so much more. There we will feel connected to our true needs and those of others, through an open heart filled with compassion and love: Life becomes a journey from the 'i' to the 'We'.

It is very hard to jump out of the cellar and right onto the rooftop without climbing the stairs one by one. Surely some people can work miracles, but most of us have to take the steps one at a time and we have to be careful not to imagine ourselves being on the rooftop while in reality our cellar still needs cleaning. Wishful thinking, telling ourselves it is all an illusion or that it is not Now, will not get us there. Working daily on our defences *will*.

I have often seen people soar to great spiritual heights and then fall back into the tenacious grip of one of the five defences, suffering strongly from ignorance of the tricks our mind plays on us. Or in PRI words: ignorant of how defences take over our perception of the present and we live from illusion.

A spiritual focus at that stage could easily lead to the strengthening of these defences. This is very sad – a path meant to lead us to the light could actually keep us locked in darkness. For example, when we are not able to apply what our spiritual teacher has told us, and we fall hopelessly into the Primary Defence *without realizing this or knowing what to do about it.* Or if our False Hope soars when we think we have found The Way, and all others are No Good and are doomed to go to hell (False Power). Or if we use our spirituality to minimize problems in our life: 'God will take care of it, I don't need to do much about it,' 'It's all an illusion, I'll just ignore it.' Or when our spiritual exercises, meditations and visualizations make us 'feel good', thereby burying our feelings under an untrue 'peace of mind'. Or fear can be in the picture, as ideas like punishment, hell and sin clearly illustrate.

When you are on a serious spiritual path, it can be very helpful to find out about the psychological immune system we were all born with, how it works and how we can dismantle it.

BODY, MIND AND SPIRIT

In their book *Living in the Spirit*, Balinese psychiatrist Luh Ketut Suryani and English psychologist Peter Wrycza present a model consisting of three concentric circles, representing, from the outside to the inside, body, mind and spirit.

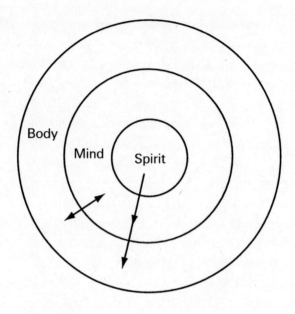

Figure 4 Relationship between and mutual influence of body, mind and spirit

The spirit is the only immutable level of our being. It is eternal and never changes. In the ancient scriptures of the Vedas the spirit is called the *Atma* or the Self. In Christian tradition it is referred to as the Soul. It is our personal connection to the Divine. Spirit cannot be influenced by anything outside us, nor by the energy of our Mind or Body. However, Spirit energy can enter and profoundly influence both Body and Mind.

The Mind in this model is defined as all of our thoughts and emotions. You can see the Mind as the individual psyche, the psychological level that we normally function from and usually identify with. The five defences belong to the realm of the Mind.

Even though the Body and the Mind levels are separate in this model, they are seen to greatly influence each other. However, they cannot enter nor influence Spirit, which is always there, changeless, eternal, immutable. On the other hand, when Mind and Body are out of balance they *can* influence our ability to connect to Spirit. An unbalanced state of Body and Mind will make it very hard, sometimes even impossible, for us to access the Spirit dimension of our being.

The level of Spirit becomes more and more accessible as the Mind and Body levels open up – are balanced, you could say. This becomes more within reach once the main blockages on the level of Body and Mind have been cleared, or, in other words, when a good deal of work on defences has helped 'clean our house'. Then the amazing level of Spirit and its connection to the much larger all-encompassing Divine domain will become available to us to experience. Not as a belief structure imposed by someone else, not as a book of rules to follow imposed by a church, not as something to daydream about or talk and hypothesize about, or read about. No, not as any of those, but *as something to experience directly for ourselves*. An experience that lies beyond the sensory, which we are accustomed to basing our lives upon. An experience beyond what we can rationalize, understand with our logical brain or talk about with words.

Beyond our senses and beyond our mind we can go 'out-of-our-mind' and experience something completely unexpected, yet so deeply familiar. When entering this domain we just need to let go of trying to grasp logically what is happening to us, stop trying to put it into words, and instead only open our hearts and surrender to it. Once we get a taste of this House of Being we will know that this is where we belong, that this is our home. However, it is hard to get there just by wishing for it or dreaming about it. We might need to fight the five defences first.

I sincerely hope that the instruments to do this have been given to you through this book.

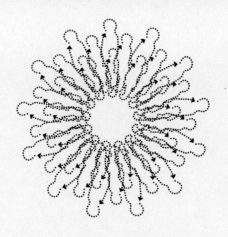

Appendix 1

Personal Defence
Profile Test

The following test helps to determine what your preferred defence mechanism is. Everyone of us engages in all five defences, but there is a difference in the frequency with which we tend to employ either one or the other defence mechanism. The following test can help you take a closer look at your defences so you can learn what your specific defence profile is.

On a scale of 1 to 10, rate the degree to which you think each statement describes you.

1 indicates not at all, 10 indicates completely (if you want you can write down the numbers that apply to you in the boxes). You can also take the test on the PRI website.

Some statements are made up of two parts. In that case be sure to rate the degree to which the *entire* statement applies to you. If one part does apply while the other doesn't, then the entire statement doesn't really apply.

In your own interests, be as honest as you can. Remember you don't have to talk to anyone else about your answers; you don't even have to tell anyone about it. It is difficult to be honest about defences because they are not our most flattering side. So search deep inside yourself for the true answer, even when you would rather not admit it, even to yourself. Remember you are now taking important steps in your own healing. If you nevertheless find that you have an irresistible urge to make your score look (just a little bit) better than is justified, remember that this signifies a defence at work.

1. *I often find myself trying to accomplish things that* ❑ *somehow don't seem to succeed.*

2. *My friends describe me as a nervous type of* ❑ *person, afraid of making mistakes.*

3. *In the beginning stage of the projects I think up,* ❑ *I usually get a lot of energy. It can feel as if my life has a purpose again.*

4. *I feel a strong need for closeness in my* ❑ *relationships.*

5. *I need a lot of attention from my partner in* ❑ *regard to my emotional life.*

6. *My colleagues know they can always count on me.* ❑ *If they need help with anything at all, I'll be there to do it for them unless I am out of my depth.*

7. *I get really tense about being able to perform* ❑ *well enough.*

8. *No matter how often I fail, I don't give up easily. I* ❑ *usually feel it's worth it to give something another try.*

9. *I usually feel I can still do better. I consider myself* ❑ *to be a perfectionist.*

10. *It isn't very difficult for me to admit to and feel* ❑ *emotional pain.*

11. *A lot of people cannot be trusted.* ❏

12. *My friends tell me I impress them, sometimes even intimidate them.* ❏

13. *I usually feel I'm controlling the situation.* ❏

14. *Sometimes it can give me a good feeling to tell people 'the truth', even in an angry way.* ❏

15. *If my partner doesn't live up to our agreements I will certainly confront him/her.* ❏

16. *I take on a lot of responsibility, but I really dislike it when others don't take theirs. I resent having to help them out because they screwed up.* ❏

17. *I generally feel quite a bit more competent than others.* ❏

18. *I get irritated easily when people screw up.* ❏

19. *People tell me that I can give them the feeling of being treated like a child.* ❏

20. *I don't feel many unpleasant emotions. Just anger and irritation on a regular basis.* ❏

21. *Even though I haven't accomplished much, I do feel successful in life.* ❏

22. *Everybody likes me, but I also hear quite often that they have a feeling that they don't really know me.* ❏

23. *My life is usually fine. Not great, but OK.* ❏

24. *I prefer spending time by myself.* ❏

25. *I don't seem to have much need for intense emotional stuff, I would rather be doing things.* ❏

26. *I help others out when they ask me, I don't feel taken advantage of easily.* ❑

27. *I don't get upset easily. I'm usually even-tempered.* ❑

28. *I don't need much.* ❑

29. *I don't have (m)any close friends.* ❑

30. *It is hard for me to get in touch with my feelings. I usually feel just OK.* ❑

31. *I usually feel inferior.* ❑

32. *Deep down I have this feeling that I'm just a bad person.* ❑

33. *No matter how successful I am, I still basically feel worthless.* ❑

34. *I often feel weighed down by the sense that I am carrying too much responsibility.* ❑

35. *To be honest I always feel that when people get to know me, they won't like me. I'm always surprised to find out that they do like me.* ❑

36. *Somehow I don't feel (worthy to be) loved, not really.* ❑

37. *I have a lot of anxiety and fear inside me.* ❑

38. *I'm afraid that if I go into therapy the therapist will find out that I'm basically no good as a person and let me know.* ❑

39. *I often feel that when things go wrong it is my fault.* ❑

40. *No matter how hard I try, it will just never be good enough.* ❑

41. *I am afraid of speaking in front of a group.* ❑

42. *I am hesitant to travel by myself.* ❑

43. *Sometimes I have sudden heart palpitations.* ❑

44. *I often experience cold sweats.* ❑

45. *I quite easily back off when confronted with loud and assertive people. They intimidate me.* ❑

46. *I have a phobia.* ❑

47. *I sometimes suffer from panic attacks.* ❑

48. *I quite often experience trembling sensations.* ❑

49. *My breathing easily gets out of control.* ❑

50. *I often experience diarrhoea.* ❑

Before you add up your score, make an educated guess at which defence you think you will score highest on, and which one will be second highest, etc. You can note this here:

1.

2.

3.

4.

5.

Answers

Next add up your scores for statements 1–10, then 11–20, then 21–30, then 31–40, and 41–50, and divide each score by 10. The highest score will show you the defence you most typically engage in, the lowest one indicates the defence you engage in least, etc.

The first 10 questions relate to False Hope, the next 10 to False Power, the next 10 to Denial of Needs, the next 10 to Primary Defence and the last 10 to Fear.

Keep observing yourself. You are now aware of your specific defence profile. The absolute score tells you something about your level of defensiveness: are you very well defended in general (scores 7, 8, 9, 10), or are you well on your way to relinquishing your defences (scores 1, 2, 3, 4)? The higher your scores, the more often you feel a need to defend yourself. This means that there are still many things that are symbolic for you. Many different situations or people will make you shift consciousness from Adult Consciousness to your defences, resulting in your being in a defence a lot of the time. In this case, beware of what you think is true about others, yourself, what you need and what is important. After all, when we are defending against the old pain we cannot trust our perceptions to be an accurate representation of the present.

In order to evaluate the progress you are making in your PRI process, redo this test every once in a while and compare your results.

NB If at the beginning of the programme you find that you have a low score on all five defences (lower than 4), remember that this signals that your Denial of Needs defence is working overtime!

➪ @ *You can find this Personal Defence Profile on the PRI site as well*

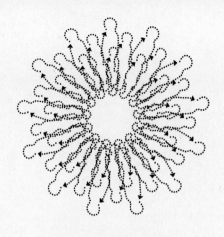

Appendix 2

Further Explanation and Examples of the Five Defences

The Five Defences: Life-saving Then, Life-threatening Now

For the children we were, the defences were necessary for our survival. For the adults we are now, defences can have disastrous effects on life.

In order to heal it is of great importance to realize how destructive it is to defend ourselves against our old pain. It is a difficult job, but relinquishing our defences is the most important aspect of the PRI healing process, a process aimed at improving the quality of our lives and the lives of those around us.

Isn't the state of being that all great spiritual teachers describe as enlightenment 'nothing more' than that: a state in which we are no longer employing any defence mechanisms? Most spiritual teachers appear to say that enlightenment is nothing out of the ordinary, that it is not something we can work towards, because it is already here. It is our natural state of being. However, we don't realize this because we are not living in the present, in the moment that is now. Instead, most of us are living mainly in the past, trapped in the illusion that that is what is happening now, making it impossible to see the present for what it truly is.

This description of what prevents us from living in our natural state of enlightenment much resembles what happens when we unconsciously see the past reality and act based upon those perceptions, while we are completely convinced that we are perceiving and acting upon the present. This is the nature of our defence mechanisms. An undivided consciousness – lacking defences – would be able to perceive fully the moment that is now every time, as described by these teachers. And isn't an undivided consciousness our natural state? The state in which we were created?

Let's take a closer look at each of the five defences. To understand what they are and how they worked when we were children, and how they function now we're adults, is the first step that will help us on the road to improving our lives.

False Hope: I Will Get What I Need, If Only I ...

The False Hope (FH) defence mechanism consists of denying the childhood truth that our needs will never be met by telling ourselves that it is possible to get them met, if we could only do or be what our parents want us to do or be: nicer or smarter or quieter or more entertaining, less emotional, more emotional, etc. However, this strategy never works because the truth is that our needs as a child were not fully met by our care-givers, no matter what we did or didn't do, were or weren't, had or didn't have, etc.

As adults, the need that we feel so strongly in the present is actually the old childhood need that never got met. So therefore, anything that we try to accomplish when we employ the False Hope (FH) defence mechanism is doomed to fail. No matter what we do, we will never be able to fulfil the need that was not met in the past. The child didn't get what she needed then, and the adult now can never do anything in the present to change that. We can't go back to change the past.

The following comparison is often helpful: Suppose that you were hungry, even starving sometimes as a child. You could eat as much as you want today, but it will never change the fact that you were starving as a child.

. . . .

Imagine Clare, who has a strong need for approval from her partner. She tries to get his approval by doing things exactly the way he wants her to. Since this is an old need, no matter what she does, Clare will never be able to get enough approval to satisfy her old need. The need will always remain, even if her partner tells her every day how glad he is that she does all these things for him. Because it is a childhood need, any appreciation he offers will not be adequate. Clare might think he doesn't really mean it and that he's just saying whatever it is he is saying to manipulate her. Or she might literally not hear him when he tells her what he thinks of her, or forget what he says rather quickly. In the end she will end up always doubting how much he appreciates her.

. . . .

The reason is so obvious, but at the same time so hard to see when we are coming from our defences: we can never satisfy an old unmet need, no matter how much it seems to be met in the present. However, since False Hope gives us a sense (albeit temporary and fleeting) of hope, it has the capacity to make us feel good as long as it lasts, which is until it inevitably crashes.

When we are in our Childhood Consciousness we will feel the old reality, the pain of the unmet need. Nothing that happens in the present adult reality will be able to change this fact or, therefore, the feeling that goes with it. We can't change the past, but we can heal its consequences on our lives now.

Examples of False Hope

- *Wearing the same clothes, reading the same books, eating the same foods, etc. as your new friend, so he will like you*

- *Taking care of everyone else's needs before taking care of your own*

- *Thinking that getting a new partner will make you much happier*

- *Thinking that losing weight will make others think you are worth their while*

- *Doing everything perfectly so nobody will get angry*

- *Hoping that moving to a bigger house will bring more happiness*

- *Buying a new car feeling that you will be more appreciated*

- *Not being able to stop working, thinking 'let's just finish up a little bit more'*

- *Trying to make a good, kind, friendly, etc. impression on others in order to get appreciation*

- *Not showing certain emotions or thoughts because you think others won't care for you any more if 'they know what you are really like'*

- *Thinking that if you just follow someone else who 'knows better', all will be fine.*

False Hope usually has a certain sense of urgency to it: 'I have to get that new kitchen now,' 'I should call her now to show how much I care,' etc. And in the end it always fails. False Hope can never give you a lasting effect. Since the real need underlying the False Hope stems from childhood, it can never be fulfilled and False Hope will always, in the end, leave you feeling unsatisfied. That's when it is time for another defence to kick in.

Denial of Needs: I Don't Have a Problem

Denial of Needs is the sort of behaviour that is aimed at avoiding any difficulty. People who engage in this defence usually come across as nice and easy-going, relaxed, not bothered by (m)any problems, in control and very evenly tempered. They often seem carefree. On the outside they seem to be quite well adjusted in an emotional and psychological sense. The only thing that is 'suspicious' is the lack of intimacy in their lives. Quite often they have few if any close friends, and they have difficulty engaging in emotional intimacy, even with their spouse and children. Mostly people who engage in this defence on a regular basis are men. Nevertheless it is important not to generalize, because there are women who will recognize their behaviour in this defence. We call this kind of defence the Denial of Needs (DN) defence mechanism.

Behind Denial of Needs there is the following drive: the denial of having a need or a problem yourself (and thus feeling vulnerable).

Denial of Needs allows us to think that we have no problems, it is just the people around us who have problems. The person who often uses the Denial of Needs defence will frequently encounter criticism concerning his incapacity to show himself, be intimate, to say what's going on with him. However, to the person criticized this criticism reflects a problem the *other* person has. He doesn't feel anything is really wrong with him or the situation. Denial of Needs also leads to forgetfulness, chronic procrastinating behaviour, avoiding taking on any responsibility and a general mental, emotional and physical numbness. All of this enables him not to feel any pain. The person who is prone to not having any problems (Denial of Needs) will often find that his life is lacking in vital energy. That a true Spark is missing. He also may be lonely because of the difficulty he has sharing himself.

Examples of Denial of Needs

- *I don't really care where we go on holiday; my husband always decides*

- *I haven't spoken to my parents in six months. That's OK, they understand*

- *I don't really care if someone treats me unkindly*

- *I will change the broken lamp tomorrow*

- *Watching a lot of TV, reading book after book, surfing the web or playing video games for hours on end, and any other activity which numbs you to yourself and the world around you*

- *Snacking – and overeating, drinking alcohol regularly, smoking, gambling and all other activities that directly numb you to your emotions.*

False Power: Nothing Is Wrong with Me, But a Lot Is Wrong with You; If Only You Would Change There Would Not Be Any Problem

The False Power (FP) defence mechanism comes across very differently. It is characterized by behaviour ranging from irritation to murderous rage and everything in between, including anger. Employment of this sort of defence is usually quite intimidating to other people and makes them rebel or, more usually, comply. We have all encountered the high-powered, authoritative, strict, demanding, vengeful, easy-to-judge-and-punish behaviour somewhere or other. Quite often we have parents who behave that way, or bosses. Often this defence is used by men. But again, here too we have to be careful not to generalize.

The person who often uses the False Power (FP) defence mechanism does feel something is wrong, but not with himself. He blames the people around him for being stupid, careless, immoral, lazy, dishonest, mean, good for nothing, out to do him harm, etc. 'Nothing is wrong with me, but everything is wrong with you (and the rest of the world),' thinks this person, who is usually convinced that he is absolutely justified in his judgements. He is not plagued by doubts about his own ideas concerning the wickedness or uselessness of others. He will feel irritation,

155

anger or even murderous rage towards others, avoiding his own vulnerability and pain – the vulnerability and pain that would rise up if he acknowledged that his needs weren't being (hadn't been) met. The angry behaviour gives people employing this defence mechanism a sense of power, it makes them feel strong, stronger than the other. This illusion of strength can actually feel very good, just as the illusion of the person employing the Denial of Needs defence mechanism has of being problem-free, feels good. So, to a certain degree, and always temporarily, the Denial of Needs and the False Power defence can, just as the False Hope defence, make us feel good.

Underneath that surface feeling there is, however, discomfort. The person who employs the False Power defence is often troubled by conflicts. She is apt to alienate those close to her by telling them she does not want them in her life any more if they don't succumb to her idea of the truth. Although False Power can temporarily make us feel good, the pain of the child we were can never be healed by acting in the present as if we are powerful over others, or as if we don't have any needs. It is not real power, it is an illusion of power, False Power, which only gives temporary relief from old pain. The pain will be brought up again and again when we inevitably confront people or situations that touch upon our old pain, and therefore the need to engage in a False Power defence will arise time and again. The result will be that we are caught in relationships with other people that are either lacking in true intimacy, or are full of conflict.

Consider John and Ingrid. John likes watching football every week and on special occasions more than once a week. Ingrid doesn't understand what he likes about it so much but she knows that 'most men like this sort of thing' and thinks that she should let him watch football when he wants. But something happens when he turns on the television. She notices irritation soaring through her body, and she starts making nasty remarks. She tells him how stupid the football game is, she asks him how he can enjoy such a Neanderthal activity, and whether he has any brains himself. John has come to accept her predictable behaviour and he doesn't say much in response. This makes Ingrid even angrier and sometimes she actually feels as if she could hit him.

In a therapy session Ingrid found out that she was using the False Power defence mechanism and so she asked herself what old pain was touched upon by John watching football (a Symbolic Situation for Ingrid). When she was able to move away from the Wall of Denial and experience her old, childhood reality, she felt the pain of being neglected emotionally. People in her family didn't pay much attention to her needs, and they were consumed with their own activities at her expense. Now every time Ingrid feels that she is less important than some other activity John is interested in, she is capable of realizing that this is the childhood reality of her old pain coming up. She can feel the pain now, and doesn't need to protect herself against it with an angry approach. She can also be open to see that she is important to John, and that his interest in football does nothing to diminish that present-day reality.

Examples of False Power

- *yelling at your children to go to bed*

- *telling your wife that you know better and she should shut up, instead of trying to understand her point of view*

- *hitting your dog*

- *getting irritated when you lose your keys*

- *ignoring your colleague because he said something that made you cross*

- *gossiping, speaking negatively about others*

- *judging other people's ideas, lifestyle, taste, habits, ideals, etc.*

- *not trusting others, thinking they are up to 'no good'*

- *feeling superior.*

Until we are able to distinguish between the old reality and the present-day reality, we will defend ourselves against feeling old pain every time a Symbol causes us to shift from our Adult Consciousness to our Childhood Consciousness and from there on to our defences.

Three of the ways we defend ourselves, False Hope, Denial of Needs and False Power, make us feel good, albeit temporarily. We can experience an enormous energy rush when our False Hope is fuelled, energy to move mountains or otherwise accomplish the impossible. False Power has similarly intoxicating effects with its illusory sense of control over people and situations. Denial of Needs makes life 'easy' because our insensitivity gives us the impression that nothing is really a problem. But inevitably the hope crashes, the power crumbles and the insensitivity can be blown apart by a sudden and overwhelming fear.

Underneath these defences there are, however, yet two other defences which we can resort to when the hope crashes or the power fades. These defences do not make us feel good at all, not even temporarily; the first one is called the Primary Defence.

Primary Defence: I'm Bad, I'm Guilty, It's All Too Much

The Primary Defence is named 'primary' because employing it is the first thing our mind does to protect us from the life-threatening pain we experience in our childhood. Employing the Primary Defence is the first thing children do to defend themselves. The Primary Defence is very simple and basic, and it is a defence mechanism employed by everyone. In the case of Denial of Needs, False Hope and False Power there is a difference in the degree to which we are prone to using one or the other. Even though we all engage in all forms of defence, our typical or outward behaviour usually shows either mostly Denial of Needs, False Hope or False Power. The Primary Defence, however, exists underneath all outside appearances, and is experienced (incorrectly) as a basic, intrinsic part of our nature by all of us.

By definition young children are helpless and dependent on others (their care-givers) to fulfil all of their needs (food, clothing, shelter, love, nurturing, safety, etc.). When those needs are not fulfilled from the outside by others, the child protects himself against this life-threatening truth by thinking he should be able to meet these needs from within. But of course the child is still too young to do this. The result is the development of negative thoughts about ourselves. 'There is something wrong with me because I cannot take care of my needs.' The child will develop the Primary Defence as soon as he has developed a sense of self-awareness. This starts around the age of 1½ to 2 years.

Examples of the Primary Defence

- *I will never be able to do it, it is too much for me*
- *I'm bad*
- *I'm just no good, I'll never be good enough*
- *I'm guilty, I am always the one who screws things up*
- *Nobody cares for me*
- *I'm worthless*
- *I'm ugly*
- *I'm not interesting*
- *I'll always be alone*
- *I'm shameful, etc.*

The Primary Defence is characterized by all beliefs, thoughts and ideas that amount to a severely negative self-evaluation. For some of us these beliefs focus more on the idea of being guilty and not good enough, ultimately leading to rejection (usually False Hope-identified people). For others the emphasis is on being an intrinsically bad person, only to be found out sooner or later by others and then rejected (usually False Power-identified people). For some the Primary Defence is more on the surface (False Hope-identification), for others it is pushed very far away (False Power-identification). Whatever the connection to our other defences or how far we've managed to push it away, the basic Primary Defence belief is 'there is something wrong with me,' most often showing up as thoughts of either 'I'm bad' or 'I'm guilty' or 'It's too much for me.'

The Primary Defence is an effective defence because when we think something is wrong with us, we don't have to feel the horror and pain of the old life-threatening reality: that our survival needs were not met. Feeling something is wrong with us prevents us from realizing that there was absolutely nothing wrong with the child we were. There was, however, something wrong with the environment we were in: the environment (usually the parents) was not able to provide the child with what he needed.

While providing an effective way to avoid clearly seeing the people around us for what they truly are, the Primary Defence also gives the child a sense of control. If the child believes that her needs are not being met because something is basically wrong with her, this implies that she could *change* the predicament she is in. She owes her predicament to herself, so therefore there is maybe something she can do to change it. Here the line between the Primary Defence and False Hope becomes very thin: the Primary Defence can easily move into becoming False Hope. Of course this will fail, but at least the children we were could live with that life-saving illusion. This is made possible because of the Primary Defence.

It is important to realize that the Primary Defence is quite a broad concept. The Primary Defence also includes feelings such as 'I can't do it, it is too much for me,' when faced with a task that need not necessarily be difficult in and of itself. This is a feeling that many of us recognize. However, it is a defence, because the reality that is being denied is the reality that we should never have had to fulfil our own needs in the first place. It was never our job to 'do it' (meet our own needs), it was our parents' job. The child should have never even have had to think about how to meet her own needs, something of which she, of course, was incapable.

Sometimes confusion is experienced over the Primary Defence. Clients note that most human beings do make mistakes, or wrong other people, and are therefore sometimes guilty of something. Therefore how could feeling guilty always be a defence? It is useful to distinguish between feeling 'I am guilty or bad' and 'I have made a mistake or done something wrong.' In the latter case the adult response is to admit openly to our fault, take responsibility, apologize and empathize if we have hurt someone's feelings, and take restorative action, if possible. This reaction is characterized by an adult sense of responsibility and proactive behaviour, and is in clear contrast to the response of feeling guilty as a person. When we feel guilty or bad we are usually passive, and try to hide what we did out of fear of punishment, instead of owning up to it openly. The idea of restorative action doesn't enter our thoughts, which are overtaken by fear. And true empathy for the other person, in the case where we've hurt someone else, is not a possibility either. Feeling guilty is not an adult response and always signifies that our

Primary Defence is operating. Admitting to a mistake and doing something about it is an adult response.

Traditional religion easily legitimizes and enforces the Primary Defence. Many religions advocate the idea that we humans are basically sinful, unworthy creatures, and only by following the religion's rules and rituals might there be hope for us. Can you see the destructive effect this can have on someone's self-perception? In other words, these religious ideas about our 'true nature' can feed right into the Primary Defence, leading to intense suffering caused by negative thoughts and feelings about ourselves. At the same time an almost insurmountable fort of defence has been erected.

> You could say that it was offered to me on a silver platter. What else could I do? I couldn't do anything but accept, I couldn't do anything but envelop myself in feelings of guilt. In this way I didn't have to feel anything else. I didn't have to feel how terribly, terribly alone I was. I only had to feel guilt. The church obliged me to feel guilt. Didn't that come in handy, my rescue? I flee in feelings of guilt. I can handle those, because the church tells me they are good. Not knowing what I'm doing to myself. With this I kill every other feeling inside me and with that I kill every bit of life in me. Then I stop being alive. Only in that way can I continue, can I survive. There is no other way. There was just one feeling that I was allowed to feel and that was guilt, I was even forced to feel it. And with that I condemn myself, so mercilessly hard, but with that I am also able to save myself.

This woman was raised in a Christian tradition. A strict Christian tradition which teaches its followers that people are sinful from the moment they are conceived; that although people do not deserve to live because of their sinful nature, people are alive and so must do penance daily; that it is vital to acknowledge just how sinful mankind is; that man should live in a continuous fear of God, that Jesus died for mankind's sins, etc. Although not all Christian traditions preach such severe concepts, the idea of being guilty by nature is a basic premise in Christianity.

A closer look at many religious or spiritual teachings often reveals these defensive tendencies: 'Our suffering is caused by our own impurity, our guilty and sinful nature. We need to be strong and do our best.' What happens to the child early in life and the influence on our feelings and behaviour when we are adults is not addressed. Emotional problems are often referred to as 'sand in the wind' – release the sand and it will blow away. This demonstrates a denial of the truth that the emotional suffering was caused during our childhood because we didn't get what we needed. The old pain won't 'blow away' until we face it, acknowledge and feel it. The idea that it will is an illustration of a Denial of Needs defence.

It is unfortunate that the blindness our society has in respect to our children's suffering, and the devastating effects this suffering has on our lives as adults, is supported by these ideas inspired by religion, be it Eastern or Western. Increasingly, however, there seems to be a tendency for people to embrace a spiritual (as opposed to religious) outlook on life that emphasizes the beauty of humanity's true nature and that sees humanity's essential quality as being nothing less than love in the divine sense of the word. This seems to be a step away from guilt-ridden religions and a step towards the message of great spiritual masters throughout the ages. Spiritual masters not linked to dogmatic, rigid, hierarchical religions based on power structures; power structures and ideas of sinfulness that provide them with power over their followers. However, as of yet, these (new) ways of thinking and practising spirituality still seem to overlook the far-reaching effects of our childhood, thereby opening the door widely to the five defences and the pain they cause us.

Fear: I Can Still Escape ...

The Primary Defence and the other defences (False Hope, False Power and Denial of Needs) can only be developed once the child has a certain level of self-awareness. This isn't the case until the age of 1½ to 2 years of age. A little baby who lies alone crying in its cot is not yet capable of thinking: 'I am a bad little baby and therefore nobody is paying any attention to my crying' (Primary Defence). Until the age of 2 the child is not capable of defending herself in a cognitive way (by thinking). Up to that time the only thing that happens when her basic needs are not met is that she will become afraid. A little baby who cries will produce stress hormones. The longer the child is left to cry alone, the more stress hormones it will produce, the more afraid it will feel. If this states persists because nobody comes to take care of the child's needs, the child will enter into a numbed state which can be compared with dissociation: the little baby will stop crying no matter how hungry, cold, wet, in pain, afraid she is ...

As adults we can recognize the working of the Fear defence mechanism when we suffer from feelings of fear in situations that are not dangerous.

Examples of Fear

- *being afraid to speak in public*
- *being scared to go to a party*
- *being afraid to speak your mind*
- *avoiding confrontation*
- *fear of spiders, mice, etc.*
- *being afraid to be alone*
- *being afraid to commit to a relationship, etc.*

This list of situations that might bring up fear, while there is not any *real* danger present, is quite endless. The reader who wants to know more about the defence of Fear might want to take a look at my earlier book, *Illusions*. In this book Fear is elaborately addressed. For now the most important point to keep in mind is to know that unrealistic fears – and most fears that afflict us are unrealistic since there is no immediate physical danger involved – serve as a defence against old pain. As long as there is fear, there is the illusion that we can still flee, that we might still be able to escape from whatever threat we perceive. This is an illusion because the child we were could not escape from its situation, the devastating situation in which its basic needs were not met.

As soon as we feel Fear when there is no real physical danger in the present, this means that a Symbol

166

has touched old pain. We avoid feeling this old pain by defending against it with Fear.

In the PRI circle I draw the Fear Defence as a kind of barbed wire, located on the border of the first cognitive defence (the Primary Defence) and Childhood Consciousness. It is as if Fear functions as a last – usually very effective – barbed-wire fence to prevent us from entering Childhood Consciousness. Fear makes us run the other way as fast as we can: into our other defences, as far away from the old pain as possible.

Just as is the case with the Primary Defence, it is very important *not to feel the Fear itself*, thinking (erroneously) that this is the old pain, which needs to be felt. Fear protects us *against* old pain and is *not* the old pain itself!

In conclusion, there are several ways of defending ourselves against childhood pain by substituting the old reality with an imaginary one: DN, FH, FP, PD, Fear. All are called denial, because their inherent nature is to deny the truth: the old reality as it really was. Every time we engage in one of the defence mechanisms, it means that old pain was touched upon by a Symbol, and we are defending ourselves against feeling that pain by believing in an illusion:

- *False Hope: I can get what I need, if I just ….*
- *Denial of Needs: I don't care/need anything, I'm fine, nothing is going on.*
- *False Power: It is your fault, you are no good, you are wrong, etc.*
- *Primary Defence: There is something wrong with me, I'm no good, it is my fault, I am guilty, I can't do it, etc.*

- *Fear: I can still escape from the danger and maybe get what I need.*

Engaging in our defences, therefore, means believing in an illusion. We believe in this illusion because the child we were could not face the pain of knowing the truth. But as an adult, believing in the illusion will only push the truth away even further behind an ever-thickening Wall of Denial and make healing less and less likely.

Please see my book *Illusions* for an extensive explanation of all defences and how to work with them. Recognizing defences is difficult because our defences are generated at an *unconscious level* – a level that we are not *by definition* aware of. The examples and practical tools in *Illusions* help to deal with this difficulty.

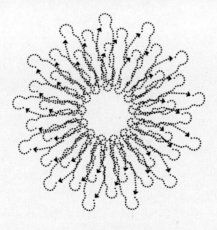

Appendix 3

Defence Recognition Test

Please take this test to see how well you are able to recognize the five defences (5 Ds). If you find that you can correctly discern which defence is manifesting through a certain behaviour, thought or emotion, you can proceed to Phase 1 of the programme. If, however, you find that you are having difficulty recognizing which one of the 5 Ds is present, please read Appendix 2 – Further Explanation and Examples of the Five Defences. If you feel a need to get more info please read my first two books – *Rediscovering the True Self* and *Illusions*.

Please read the following statements and note whether you think they represent Denial of Needs, False Hope, False Power, Primary Defence, or Fear. (Answers are on page 173.)

1. *I can't help trying to explain my spiritual experiences to my husband even after he has made it clear that he can't and won't understand.*

2. *I have to help her; if I give up she won't make it.*

3. *I'm always doing my best to be nice so I won't get into trouble with her.*

4. *I always feel inferior at work with my colleagues. I'm inhibited during meetings about saying what is really on my mind.*

5. *I'm often panicky when I have to speak in front of a group.*

6. *I can't stand how stupid these people are. Why don't they do their homework and prepare properly?*

7. *I'm sure nobody really cares whether I'm there or not, I never have anything interesting to say anyway.*

8. *I just don't want to be bothered when I come home from work, I want to read my newspaper, watch sports, have a beer and relax.*

9. *It's fine if my friends forget my birthday. Hey, I'll have a good time anyway.*

10. *The world has become a bad place, people can't be trusted and they only think of themselves anyway.*

11. *I always get blamed. I hate them for doing that to me.*

12. *I can manage by myself. I have to; nobody else will do it for me.*

13. *It's useless digging up the past, it's over. Put it behind you and get on with your life.*

14. *I always take on too much responsibility and hope they will appreciate me, but I wonder if they really notice.*

15. *My childhood was the way it was because I chose it to be like that. It is my karma. I'm grateful to my parents for the abuse.*

Answers

1. FH
2. FH
3. FH
4. PD
5. Fear
6. FP
7. PD
8. DN
9. DN
10. FP
11. FP
12. FP
13. DN
14. FH
15. DN

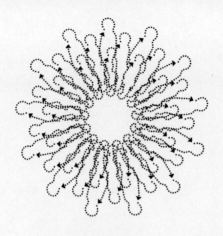

Appendix 4

Breathing Techniques: Getting in Touch with Your Body, Calming Fear and Stress

Breathing and Creating Body Awareness
– Denial of Needs

Some people have lived in Denial of Needs for such a long time that they can find it extremely difficult to know *what* they are feeling, or even *that* they are feeling anything at all. Their Denial of Needs defence has worked so well since early childhood that recognizing a defence – an emotional reaction, after all – is very challenging. On top of that, in the rare case that they manage to signal a defence, it will be extremely hard to dissect it into the Sensory Perception and the Meaning, because to do that we need to be in touch with our feelings. We cannot get to the Sensory Perception, and especially not to the Meaning, if we are not in touch with our feelings.

If you find you are having this difficulty, I suggest you try doing the following breathing exercise. You will discover that breathing is *the link* between your mind and your body. Becoming aware of your breathing and training yourself to breathe in a specific way will let you get in touch once more with your body and, as a consequence, with your feelings.

Feelings are located in your body, not in your head. To illustrate this point I remember a client with a great deal of Denial of Needs who once told me that he used to think that his feelings were in his head. One day he heard that a friend of his had died. In his head he said to himself, 'That is really sad.' He thought this specific thought was actually his 'feeling'. He did not cry. He did notice a vague sort of stomach ache, but figured he might have had something to eat that was upsetting his stomach. Later on he realized that the feeling in his stomach was actually his feeling of sadness over the death of his friend. It was quite a discovery for him that feelings actually are always to be felt *in the body.* What you have in your mind are thoughts, not feelings. Even when those thoughts might be *about* feelings, that still does not make them into feelings. As he described it himself, he used to live as if his head were separate from his body, the contact between the two having been severed.

Breathing can help enormously to restore this contact.

Try to do the following exercise for a couple of minutes as often as you think of it, but at least three times a day:

- *Breathe out slowly. Squeeze out almost all the air by tensing your stomach muscles and pushing in your stomach. Take about 6 seconds in total to breathe out like this.*

- *Then relax your stomach muscles. As you do that the air will automatically gush into your lungs again. Take about 4 seconds to breathe in this way and then start breathing out again.*

If you do this several times a day you will become trained to focus on your breathing and your body more often. While breathing out your focus is on your stomach; while breathing in your focus is on your diaphragm. You will start to feel the air streaming in and out of your body. You will become aware of the path the air follows in your body: from your nose, through your throat, to your lungs, down to your stomach and maybe even into your pelvis. You will start to become aware of how your body is feeling: tense or relaxed, full of energy or tired, cold or warm, vibrant or stagnant. And, depending on the emotional situation, you will become aware of specific feelings in specific places: a flutter in your heart area, pressure on your heart, a knot in your stomach, a lump in your throat, tense shoulders and neck, etc.

Give yourself some time and you will find that with this easy breathing exercise your body and its feelings will start to open up to you, offering you the possibility of engaging with PRI much more effectively.

Breathing and Fear

When you are feeling strong fear or even panic it can be quite hard to realize you are caught in a defence, since all you will be thinking about is 'How can I get myself out of here?' Once fear kicks in, you are in a survival mode – only concerned with getting through and especially *away from* the fearful event. Even harder than recognizing that what you are feeling is a defence is to take the time to look for the Symbol and dissect it, or to remember the Defence Reversal steps, let alone apply them. Intense fear, as is the case with phobias or panic attacks, needs to be toned down a bit first in order for any other process to become possible.

Breathing is the miracle instrument. Breathing in the way described for dealing with Denial of Needs will help you quickly get out of the extreme fear. Only then will you get back in touch with your body and have some brain capacity available to examine what is happening: what Symbol started the fear response and how can I work with the defence?

- *Train yourself to breathe out for as long as possible. Put all of your attention on the exhale.*

- *Let the inhale take care of itself: it will be relatively fast and short, brought on simply by relaxing your stomach muscles. Then focus on breathing out again for as long as possible.*

The thing to remember is that breathing in activates us and breathing out relaxes us. When experiencing fear we are obviously 'over-activated', unless there is real danger, in which case the fear sets off our natural fight-or-flight response. So by breathing out for much longer than we breathe in we can help our system to relax. Once you get this technique down, you'll be amazed by its almost instantaneous effect.

The only thing that you have to focus on now is *remembering* this breathing technique when you are confronted by fear. Which sounds easier than it actually is. You can achieve this by repeating to yourself many times per day 'fear – breath', 'fear – breath', 'fear – breath'. The power of repetition will lead to you remembering to apply this breathing technique the next time fear actually grabs a hold of you. *Then you will be able to take the PRI steps, enabling you to see your fears for what they truly are: illusions.*

Breathing and Stress

All stress and stress-related afflictions can be easily influenced by the above simple breathing technique. Stress and its related problems (insomnia, high blood pressure, overeating, chronic fatigue/ME, RSI, burnout, fibromyalgia, etc.) are a result of our system being more or less permanently in a state of over-arousal, which is meant to generate a fight-or-flight response. But if there is no immediate danger to fight against or to flee from, we end up being stuck with all those stress hormones in our body. Again our breathing is our 'miracle-worker'. Apply the breathing technique regularly and you will find that your body is going to get the message that it doesn't need to be prepared for the worst all the time.

Of course, everything depends on constant and regular practice, but if you succeed, you will get the results. Then, applying PRI will also become a lot easier and more effective.

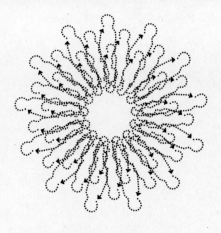

Appendix 5

The Art of Holistic Living

When looking back on my own personal development, that of my students and PRI clients in general, I have noticed that an overall – holistic – healthier way of life automatically follows from working with defensive emotions, thoughts and behaviour. The less people are living in the illusion of their defences, the stronger their need will become to develop a healthier, more aware and balanced lifestyle. For example, they often spontaneously start feeling a need to spend more time in Nature, to exercise and eat more healthily, cutting down on the intake of animal proteins, fat, sugar and alcohol, etc. Changing their lifestyle in this way makes them feel physically and emotionally more fit, setting in motion a positive self-reinforcing circle of feeling better, living more healthily and becoming less and less defensive.

The reverse holds true as well. Especially when the Primary Defence hits, we often feel a craving for fattier, unhealthy foods. We could easily reach for that extra glass of wine, bowl of ice cream or bag of crisps. Instead of heading outdoors for a nice stroll under the evening skies, we will prefer to stay indoors in front of the TV or at the computer. And consequently the drive to halt a runaway defence will be greatly diminished as well. Why get all excited, let alone worry about one defence more or less? The longer we remain within this negative spiral, the more difficult it becomes to spin free of its grip.

Giving people information on what to do and what not to do when it comes to overall lifestyle choices is a tricky business. Following up the advice might prove to be harder than we had hoped, and when we fail in our own eyes, this will just lead to an inflated Primary Defence: 'I am no good, I can't even stick to these few simple changes in my eating habits, I am such a loser.' This in turn could easily lead to: 'I don't care, never mind, I just want to drink my glass(es) of wine again.'

This realistic risk would prompt me not to give any advice on a healthier, more aware lifestyle. Also, as we all know, people start living a healthier lifestyle all by themselves, if they do their emotional work. So why go into practical tips and hints at all? Why not let people find out for themselves, as I know they surely will, sooner or later? Instead of running the highly realistic risk of activating Primary Defences ('I can never do it'), or any other defence (F#@!! this...), for that matter.

I have noticed, though, that people can be unaware of the enormous influence their lifestyle has on them, on how they feel and subsequently on how well they can apply PRI, take their emotional wellbeing into their own hands and live life to the fullest.

I will not elaborate on the points addressed here. There are people who are much more qualified to do so. And I don't want to put pressure on you. However, I would like to share with you a few aspects of a holistic lifestyle that I have found to be of much help.

1. Smoking – I never knew it when I smoked (a lot) myself, but smoking is something that is not only destructive physically (we all know about that one) but is also an enormous suppressor of feelings. This is much less well known. Consider giving it up; you will access your feelings much more easily and get ahead in your PRI work.

2. Drinking – Having a (few) drink(s) every day has become normal for many people, and I used to be one of them. I found that I was too attached to my 'little glass of wine' and that I quite missed it if I didn't have it. So after going back and forth for some years, I decided to stop it altogether. The amount of energy this gives me both in the morning as well as in the evening is incredible. Not to mention how the full experience of life, of the NOW, becomes more and more within reach when we stop numbing ourselves by using alcohol on a regular basis.

3. Recreational and medicinal drugs – just try not to use them, I would simply say. Recreational drugs, just like alcohol, will take you away from the NOW. Many medicinal drugs have the same effect. Maybe you will find that you are able to 'wait out' a little headache or muscle ache. Did you ever notice that the more painkillers we use, the more pain our body seems to produce in return and the more painkillers we need? See if yoga, Tai Chi, meditation, breathing exercises or walking in Nature can help you, without having the unwanted side-effects of drugs that have an immediate 'effect' but at a high price, such as Valium, painkillers, marijuana or sleeping pills.

In some French hospitals, breathing techniques[1] have actually become the preferred treatment for people with high blood pressure instead of giving them the usual pills.

Of course, sometimes we do need medication and it is great that these drugs are there. Just be wise in how you use them, avoiding them as much and for as long as you can.

4. Eating animals – feeding myself in a healthy way without an animal needing to be killed is not only good for the animal and for my conscience, it also is very good for my omega 3 and omega 6 rate. Not eating meat means a substantially lower intake of unhealthy omega 6 fatty acids and therefore a substantially lowered need to balance out the harmful effects thereof by taking omega 3 pills or eating fatty fish. Not to mention the way in which animals are treated in the 'modern' meat industry, one of the greatest cruelties committed by humankind. A cruelty on a massive scale, that goes on day in, day out and remains unseen and unthought-of by most of us.

The next time you see 'industry meat' in the supermarket, you might wonder about the degree of suffering you are actually looking at. Like more and more people, you might not want to put that on your plate or into your body any more.

As my 12-year-old daughter put it, 'People are becoming aware of all the animal suffering that was needed to produce that tasty bite of food in their mouth.' My daughter became a strict vegetarian the day she saw a rabbit being dissected at school. That was the moment that she became instantly aware of all the suffering[2] that is so well hidden when it comes to our food. Until that moment she had always told me, 'I want to eat meat, because it tastes so good.' In the words of a great spiritual teacher, 'Everyone should lead their life so that no pain is caused by them to any living being. That is the supreme duty.'

One last argument regarding stopping eating animals: if, like most people nowadays, you want to help our planet's environment, it is good to know that not eating meat is *one of the most effective things you can do*. Just think of all the food and water needed to raise cattle, and the large amounts of toxins that are put into the environment as waste products.

5. Eating organic – eating foods that have not been created in a factory, not artificially flavoured and coloured, not filled with preservatives nor saturated with other additives that are harmful to us, not only helps to give the body good nutrients, but also helps considerably in decreasing the vast amounts of chemicals and poisons used in the agricultural industry. When my children want to go to a fast food restaurant I tell them from my heart, 'I love you too much to feed you poison.' I'm sure many of you have had the same idea.

6. Exercise – this is a tough one. We all know how good we feel after exercise, even if it is only 15 minutes per day. But we also know how hard it is to get ourselves going. Try to find something you enjoy and make sure it is close and easily available. Going to a gym might be harder than going to your cellar or the park next door. Put on your favourite music and see if you can fit the exercise into your daily routine. Much research has shown the overwhelmingly positive effects of exercise on both body and mind.

7. Computers and TV – here we go again. Try to avoid them as much as possible when it comes to your free time. The more people watch TV, the more violent their image of the world is. The more time spent in front of a screen, the more overweight children tend to be. Not to forget the general numbing effect frequent use of either can have on us and our children, as well as a tendency to increase aggression, which has been shown in research, etc.

It is quite unusual to have this standpoint in our culture, where watching TV and playing games on the computer have become as normal as driving a car. However, all people who have 'kicked the habit' (it is a form of addiction in many cases) really enjoy their 'screen-free life' a lot better. It often feels as if they have 'taken their life back into their own hands', instead of zapping or beeping it away behind some machine.

Try it out for yourself and see what changes happen for you after a few weeks.

8. Meditation – meditation is one of the most powerful tools to influence our state of being from within. In all Eastern traditions it plays a paramount role. In contemporary medical clinics it is becoming more and more integrated, as its benefits have been shown again and again in research. Meditation can give us enormous energy, it can profoundly relax us, it can help us get in touch with deep layers of ourselves that we didn't know existed, it can lead us to feelings of bliss that we never could have dreamed about, it can help to heal our emotional and physical ailments, it can improve our concentration, it can centre us more and more inside ourselves, letting us get to know ourselves, helping us to stop running after ephemeral things in the world around us.

BUT ... I have also seen how easy it can be to go-and-sit-on-some-uncomfortable-feeling and 'meditate it away'. Be careful not to use meditation in that way. Dealing with unpleasant feelings is necessary to prevent them from just coming right back again after our meditation. Of course, the temptation is there to use meditation as a way to feel better, to wind down and to put away the discomfort probably brought about by a Symbol and a defence. Using meditation as a way to calm down and avoid problems, instead of facing them directly, is a Denial of Needs defence. Once you are aware of this you won't need to fall into this meditation pitfall.

When meditating, ask yourself before you start 'How am I feeling?' If you are not feeling good, then find out what is happening. Which defence got the better of you? You can meditate on the defence and how you got into it, if you want to. But take care not to try to 'meditate the problem away' by thinking of something soothing or using any other technique that will only temporarily suppress the current problem that needs to be dealt with, or denies that a defence has been activated and is waiting to be reversed.

Then, once you feel 'clean', free from defences, let yourself be carried into the depths of your inner being to the divine universe of the heart and beyond.

It goes without saying that all aspects of our life – physical, mental, emotional, spiritual – are intricately linked to one another. Any work you do on one level will inevitably affect the others, in a positive or a negative way, depending on whether your action was a positive one – like stopping drugs – or a negative one – like eating unhealthy foods.

Also keep in mind that changes which we make on a non-physical level in general are quicker to produce changes on the physical level than vice versa. In other words, healthy food, exercise, etc. are great for your emotional state of mind, but if for example you suffer from a resilient Primary Defence, chances are that your new food and exercise habits will fall away after a time. If you are subject to a Primary Defence, in spite of putting all your willpower into it, it will be almost impossible to hold up your good new eating and exercise habits. This then will strengthen your Primary Defence once more.

The reverse strategy is more interesting. If you truly feel good about yourself and life because you have managed to get a grip on your Primary Defence (you recognize it, you are able to find the moment it started, you know how to reverse it, you can feel the pain that is hidden behind it), then chances are high that you will not want to overeat any more or spend your evenings in front of the TV. This effect is not down to willpower, but to intrinsic motivation that will follow automatically from your emotional progress.

Good luck to you. Just remember that once you get a grip on your defences, you will automatically find that many changes will start taking place. Not for a little while. Not thanks to willpower, but to a deep change that is taking place in you. Helping you to cross over from a place called 'survival' to a territory named 'the present'.

Silver-coloured wings
Transparent as the look of a newborn child
Joyous like a brisk foal
Filled with surrender as a child that knows himself to be God
Beyond the confines of form and time
For ever in our heart

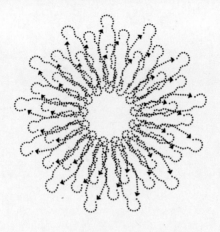

Appendix 6

Finding a PRI Therapist

Individual Therapy

At the time of writing this book (2011), PRI is available in Holland, France and Belgium. As the professional training programme is now open to therapists of any nationality, provided they speak English, PRI will soon become available in other countries as well.

Intensive Programmes

There are opportunities to undertake an *Intensive (individual, five-day) programme* with Ingeborg Bosch in the south of France. Please visit the PRI website for further details.

Assistance by Telephone

Quite a lot of PRI therapy and coaching is given by telephone, since people from all over the world seek this therapy and have no PRI therapist close by. This may sound surprising at first, but experience shows that it works quite well. A first step is to arrange a face-to-face meeting if at all possible, after which working by phone is easier. With new technologies, however, an online face-to-face meeting has become a possibility as well. At present PRI therapy by qualified PRI therapists is offered in the following languages: English, Dutch, French, German, Spanish and Italian. All qualified PRI therapists can be found on the PRI website.

Individual PRI Self-help Coaching

You can get specific individual help from a PRI therapist aimed completely at applying the three phases described in this book. This individual coaching programme consists of six sessions. The therapist will explain the phases to you and help you to practise the exercises as described. If you then decide you would like to pursue a more in-depth PRI process, you can always choose to continue with PRI therapy.

Group PRI Self-help Coaching

In a total of four evenings you will get help in a group from specially trained PRI Self-help Coaches in applying the phases and instruments described in this book. Please look on the PRI website for dates and places of these PRI Self-help Coaching evenings.

Another option would be to seek a professional counsellor or therapist in your area to see if he or she is willing to work through this book with you and maybe involve material I've provided in my other books. If the therapist has done considerable work on his or her own childhood and has a basic mental and emotional understanding of the extent of suffering children go through, you might come quite a long way. The reason that I am a little careful in advising you to work with a therapist who has not had full PRI training is that recognition of defences is quite hard for all of us, even for experienced professionals. A therapist can only take clients as far as he or she has gone him- or herself. In other words, if you end up working with a therapist who thinks he or she is aware of his or her defences but has not had full PRI training, there may be quite a few defences left of which he or she is not aware. This applies especially to those therapists who have had only partial PRI training. Inevitably this fact will influence the work he or she does with you.

Last but not least, readers do manage to apply PRI all by themselves with only the books as their aid, and have been able to achieve remarkable results. Even the worst pains from childhood and the most tenacious defences have been able to be healed in this way.

➪ *@ New developments on the availability of PRI will be made public through the PRI website:*
www.PastRealityIntegration.com

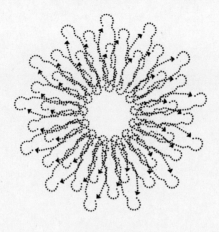

Appendix 7

For Therapists Who Want to Learn More about PRI

PRI Professional Training Programme

The full four-year professional PRI training programme has been available in English since 2010. The four-year programme for professionals consists of three training weeks per year that take place in the south of France.

PRI Introductory Workshop for Professionals

Therapists interested in the four-year training programme can start by participating in a 2½-day PRI Introductory Workshop, organized annually. These workshops are conducted in English. After this workshop it is possible to apply for the professional training programme. Please see the PRI website for both further details and online registration (www.PastRealityIntegration.com).

NB In the case of a special request for a PRI Introductory Workshop by a group of therapists (a minimum of 15) from the same country/region, it is possible to make a special arrangement so that a PRI workshop can be organized in your local area.

PRI Self-help Coach Training Programme

A special training programme for PRI Self-help Coaches is currently being developed. Please see the PRI website for further details. The PRI Self-help Coach cannot tutor people individually, nor offer to give PRI therapy. He or she is able to help people in a group setting to apply the tools of PRI Phases 1, 2 and 3 from this book. To qualify for this training programme you need to have at least two years' experience as a coach or other kind of 'health worker'. It is also essential to have undertaken your own successful individual PRI therapy. On average this takes about 35 sessions.

PRI Self-help Coaches cannot give PRI in an individual setting due to their more superficial level of PRI training and skills. In order to use PRI with clients on a one-to-one basis, it is necessary to follow the professional training programme and become a certified PRI therapist.

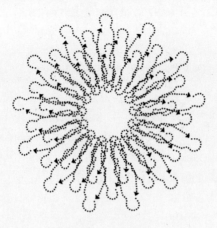

Glossary

Adult Consciousness (AC)

From this consciousness we are able to perceive the present-day situation for what it truly is. Our perception of what is happening is not coloured or dominated by past experiences, but originates from a state of inner autonomy.

Childhood Consciousness (CC)

When we experience reality from this perspective, as is the case when our defences are active, we are unable to perceive the present for what it is. Instead we experience present events in the same way as we experienced events in our early childhood. We are usually not aware that this is happening. CC consists of all our old pain put together with the defences we have developed against feeling that old pain.

Defences/Defence Mechanism/Defence System

The denial of the truth is done through our defences. There are three different kinds of illusions that seek to protect us: False Hope, False Power, and the Primary Defence. Together these constitute our defence system. Each defence entails a different way of denying what is true, and so ensures that the devastating pain doesn't break through into consciousness. As children we first develop these defences. As adults we still feel we need them, although we truly do not.

Denial

In order to make sure that the truth and the accompanying pain do not creep up on us and threaten our life, we construct a new 'reality' to replace the real one. This new 'reality' denies the real one and so helps to secure the repression of the truth.

Denial of Needs (DN)

This defence denies the truth because when we employ it we believe we don't have any unmet needs. It is characterized by behaviour that is aimed at avoiding difficulties and conflicts.

False Hope (FH)

This defence (way of denying the old truth) is characterized by thinking that it is possible to get old needs met if only we do or don't do a specific thing. This defence can be recognized by behaviour that involves keeping on trying to accomplish something that can never succeed. Instead of facing the old, painful reality, we feel hopeful in the present reality.

False Power (FP)

This defence can be recognized by behaviour that is either aggressive or intimidating. Instead of feeling the old, painful reality, we feel powerful, or in control in the present reality.

Fear

This defence convinces us that there is a present danger to flee from or defend against, hiding the truth that the danger has long since passed and that when it was present – during our childhood – there was no way to escape from it.

Old Pain (OP)

The result of needs not being met is immense pain. The pain that results from childhood needs not being met is called old pain. When we are children this pain is too big for us to feel, therefore in order to survive we need to repress it. All of our old pain put together makes up our Childhood Consciousness.

Old Unmet Needs (OUN)

As children we all had needs that were not met by our care-givers. Usually these unmet needs were of a non-physical nature (safety, respect, trust, support, etc). There are also unmet needs of a physical nature (sexual integrity and bodily safety). It is these unmet needs that make it necessary for children to hide the truth from themselves: that their needs are not being met and will never be met.

Primary Defence (PD)

This defence denies the truth by making us believe that we do not deserve to get our needs met. We feel bad, guilty, stupid, worthless, etc. This preoccupation with our own shortcomings prevents us from being able to look at what has happened to us or to look at who inflicted that on us. Instead of facing the old, painful reality, we feel bad about ourselves in the present and believe our pain is our own fault.

Repression

Because of the immensity of the old pain and because of the life-threatening reality behind it (that our needs will never be met), the children we were had to repress both the pain and the meaning behind the pain. This happens without conscious awareness. We are not aware that we use repression, nor are we aware of what we have repressed.

Suppression

In contrast to repression, suppression is a conscious act. When feelings or thoughts come up that we do not want to confront, we can choose purposely to suppress them, for example by distracting ourselves with doing something, drinking, smoking, etc. All the while, however, we are more or less aware that we are suppressing something that disturbs us.

Symbol (S)

A person or situation that reminds us of our childhood without us being consciously aware of this. For something to remind us unconsciously of the past it either closely resembles the past or is exactly the opposite of the old reality. A Symbol causes us to switch from AC to CC.

Trigger

Another word for Symbol is trigger. However, in PRI the word Symbol is preferable, because that word represents the essential nature of the experience – it symbolizes something from another time.

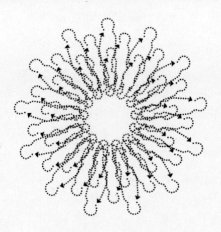

References

Foreword

1. Sri Aurobindo was the father of Indian independence, and the inspiration for Mahatma Gandhi. Having been put in prison by the British, he had a very intense spiritual experience. In the second part of his life he wrote and meditated intensely on humanity's transformation towards a new level of consciousness, which he calls the 'Supramental'. He is author of many books on this path to the Supramental. 'The Mother', his spiritual partner, a French woman also extremely advanced in spiritual development, founded Auroville in Pondicherry (southern India) in 1968. Auroville was created as a first incarnation of this new level of consciousness. Its population is now around 2,000 people. With 44 different nationalities it is a truly international place.

2. From the Vedas – the oldest holy scriptures known to humanity, believed to date back more than 4,000 years. Received and transmitted by holy men of the time in

209

India, they are the basis for the science of yoga (the path to divine union), later developing into Hinduism (1500 BC) and later still into Buddhism (600 BC).

Introduction

1. Daniel Goleman writes (*Emotional Intelligence*, Bantam Books, 1995, p. 22): 'The emotional brain's imprecision in such moments is added to by the fact that many potent emotional memories date from the first years of life, in the relationship between an infant and its caretakers. This is especially true for traumatic events, like beatings or outright neglect. During this early period of life other brain structures, particularly the hippocampus, which is crucial for narrative memories, and the neocortex, seat of rational thought, have yet to become fully developed. In memory, the amygdala and hippocampus work hand-in-hand; each stores and retrieves its special information independently. While the hippocampus retrieves information, the amyglada, which matures very quickly in the infant's brain, is much closer to fully formed at birth. LeDoux turns to the role of the amygdala in childhood to support what has long been a basic tenet of psychosomatic thought: that the interactions of life's earliest years lay down a set of emotional lessons based on the attunement and upsets in the contact between the infant and caretakers. These emotional lessons are so potent and yet so difficult to understand from the vantage point of adult life because, believes LeDoux, they are stored in the amygdala as rough, wordless blueprints for emotional life. Since these earliest emotional memories are established at

a time before infants have words for their experience, when these emotional memories are triggered in later life there is no matching set of articulated thoughts about the response that takes us over. One reason we can be so baffled by our emotional outbursts, then, is that they often date from a time early in our lives when things were bewildering and we did not yet have words for comprehending events. We may have the chaotic feelings, but not the words for the memories that formed them.'
2. Dutch and English editions. In 2005 a French and in 2008 an Italian edition were published.
3. Dutch edition. In 2007 a French edition was published. German and English editions are due out in 2014.
4. Dutch edition.
5. Longitudinal research conducted by the University of Maastricht.

Some Basic Theory

1. See Appendix 2 and *Illusions* for an in-depth exploration of the defences.

Phase 1

1. Ingeborg Bosch, 2003.

Phase 3

1. Please refer to *Illusions* where an elaborate explanation of this process makes up about 75 per cent of the book.

2. Of course these steps do not apply when you (or someone you are responsible for) are in actual physical or financial danger. In that case you need to take appropriate action in the present to ensure your safety.

Case Histories

1. Since 2005 the University of Maastricht has been doing research into PRI. In 2008 the first quantitative research began to evaluate PRI therapy's effect. At the time of writing the first results are very promising. More results and scientific publications will become available in the future.

The Art of Conscious Living

1. Seema M. Dewan, *Sai Darshan* (Hyderabad: Sree Prasanthi Publications Trust, 1999).

Appendix 5

1. Cardiac coherence – an easy breathing technique used to harmonize the cardiac rhythm.
2. Have you ever realized that it takes a fish 20 minutes to suffocate to death?

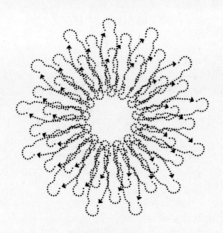

Index

Page numbers in **bold** indicate definitions

and Primary Defence 160,
161
questions to test 140
recognition 24
Sensory Perception 45–6
False Power **205**
case histories 96–9, 105–
7, 107–10, 110–13
Defence Reversal 79–82
effect of 10, 155–9
examples 29, 30–1, 40–1,
81–2, 157–8
Meaning identification 52
and Primary Defence
160–1
questions to test 140–1
risk in search for Meaning
49–50
recognition 24
Sensory Perception 38–9,
40–1
families
assistance 95
relationships 95–6, 104,
108–10, 112
Fear **205**
and breathing exercises
179–81
case histories 94–6, 100–
2, 110–13, 113–17
as defence mechanism 8
Defence Reversal 70–3
effects of 165–6
examples 30, 41–2, 44,
72–3, 143
of future event 47–8
Meaning identification 53,
54, 56
questions to test 143

recognition 23
relationship with pain 167
response to xvii
Sensory Perception 41–2,
44, 46–7
see also phobias
feelings
connecting with 178–9
control of xxvii
and meditation 191
reduced in Denial of Needs
11
effect of smoking 189
see also emotional brain;
emotional memories;
emotions
fight-or-flight (survival)
response
and stress 181
triggers xvi
freedom, from defences
68–9
friends
relationships with 38, 45–
6, 50, 55, 75–6, 152
sharing programme with
31

gambling 155
Goleman, Daniel xxiv–xxv,
210–11
gratitude 127–9
guilt 162–3

healthy lifestyle 183–92
holistic living 183–92
husbands, relationships with
xvii, 1–2, 42, 44, 53–4,
81–2, 107–10

Hay House Titles of Related Interest

JOIN THE HAY HOUSE FAMILY

As the leading self-help, mind, body and spirit publisher in the UK, we'd like to welcome you to our family so that you can enjoy all the benefits our website has to offer.

 EXTRACTS from a selection of your favourite author titles

 COMPETITIONS, PRIZES & SPECIAL OFFERS Win extracts, money off, downloads and so much more

 LISTEN to a range of radio interviews and our latest audio publications

 CELEBRATE YOUR BIRTHDAY An inspiring gift will be sent your way

 **LATEST NEWS** Keep up with the latest news from and about our authors

 ATTEND OUR AUTHOR EVENTS Be the first to hear about our author events

 iPHONE APPS Download your favourite app for your iPhone

 HAY HOUSE INFORMATION Ask us anything, all enquiries answered

join us online at **www.hayhouse.co.uk**

 292B Kensal Road, London W10 5BE
T: 020 8962 1230 E: info@hayhouse.co.uk

ABOUT THE AUTHOR

© Emilie Guilbert

Ingeborg N. Bosch (b. 1960), born in Iran to Dutch parents, received her Dutch *Doctoraal* degree (equivalent to a qualification between Master's level and PhD) in Psychology from the University of Amsterdam (1986). During her studies she took Eastern Philosophy as a minor subject; in particular the teachings of Zen Buddhism, Hua-Yen Buddhism and Taoism. The subject of her final research concentrated on Behaviour Modification techniques applied to a primary school setting. The results attracted national media attention.

Ingeborg initially worked as an independent career counsellor and management consultant, and in 1989 wrote and presented an educational television and radio series about looking for employment. As she became more and more engaged in coaching and helping individuals to function in a healthier and happier way, she encountered Alice Miller's work, while working on processing her own childhood pains. She was so gripped by the ideas in Miller's books that she started working on the basis of those ideas, focusing more and more on giving therapy.

Ingeborg went on to discover the work of Jean Jenson, who became a close colleague and taught her the therapeutic techniques that formed the basis of her own, adapted form of primal therapy. Working closely with Jenson, it was possible for Ingeborg to develop new insights and theoretical concepts which have now given rise to a fundamentally renewed therapy, PRI.

Currently operating from the south of France, Ingeborg is exclusively involved with PRI in all its different aspects. Apart from providing therapy and writing books she is dedicated to the training of therapists in order to make PRI more and more accessible to the public at large.

www.PastRealityIntegration.com